You may have special questions
about your wedding....

• What if the bride's or groom's parents are divorced?

• What if you want to write your own vows?

• What if the bridal gown must conceal a pregnancy?

• What if a death in the family necessitates postponement?

• What if former in-laws are invited?

• What if a bridesmaid can't afford a special dress?

THE COMPLETE WEDDING PLANNER
can help you over all the hurdles!

Edith Gilbert, the author, is president of Jet'iquette, a consultation service on modern etiquette. She has also written *All About Parties, Let's Set the Table, Tabletop: The Right Way,* and *Summer Resort Life.*

THE

Complete

Wedding

Planner

A PRACTICAL GUIDE
FOR THE BRIDE AND GROOM

by Edith Gilbert

WARNER BOOKS

A Warner Communications Company

A special thanks to *Washington Whirl Around* for their invaluable advice and permission to use their artwork.

Warner Books Edition

This Warner Books edition is published by arrangement with Frederick Fell Publishers, Inc., 386 Park Avenue South, New York, New York 10016.

Warner Books, Inc., 666 Fifth Avenue, New York, NY 10103

 A Warner Communications Company

Printed in the United States of America

First Warner printing: April 1984
10 9 8 7 6 5 4 3 2 1

Designed by A. Christopher Simon

Library of Congress Cataloging in Publication Data
Gilbert, Edith.
    The complete wedding planner.

    Reprint. Originally published: New York, N.Y.:
Fell Publishers, © 1983.
    Includes index.
    1. Weddings—Planning.   I. Title.
HQ745.G54   1984   395'.22   83-21635
ISBN 0-446-37322-2 (U.S.A.)
      0-446-37877-1 (Canada)

Contents

How to Use This Book

Love does not consist in gazing at each other, but in looking outward in the same direction.

ANTOINE DE SAINT-EXUPÉRY

The Complete Wedding Planner is the first book to address both the bride and the groom as a couple, and it is my desire to share with you both the most complete, up-to-date, and detailed information on the entire subject of weddings.

No matter what your age, your background, or your career or whether you have been married before (30 percent of today's marriages are second weddings), what you want to know about your forthcoming marriage is when to have the wedding, where to have it, who will officiate, how many guests to invite, what to wear, why to have a rehearsal, and how much the reception will cost. On top of all that, you want everything to go smoothly without any hassle.

In order to use the information in this book effectively, I suggest that you actively underline the sections that fit your special needs. Add any comment you wish—yes!, no!, or maybe? Then let your partner do the same with a different color ink. When you are done the book will be well marked, it's true, but you will have reached numerous important decisions jointly, and the two of you will have an accurate record for quick reference.

If your family is like most families these days, the bride and groom and their parents may be separated by large geographic distances. To make communications simpler, I can envision some parents or members of the wedding party owning their own copy of this book. Saving the price of one telephone call may cover the cost of that extra copy.

It's time now to knuckle down with a pen in hand and make plans for that perfect wedding, remembering that all weddings are the same, but none are alike! My personal wish is that all your private dreams may come true!

CHAPTER 1

Getting Off to a Good Start

Manners are the happy way of doing things.

RALPH WALDO EMERSON

Your wedding is going to be the loveliest, smoothest, most memorable wedding ever—just the kind you both always dreamed it would be! Calm, cool, and confident is the way to feel as you prepare for this happy day!

A wedding is not only a joyous occasion to share with family and friends, but it is also an important ceremonial event and as such follows a prescribed form. In spite of some restrictions, you may be surprised and delighted at the great variety of choices open to every prospective bride and groom. Many decisions will reflect your personal tastes, and consequently your wedding will be unlike any other, while still essentially following tradition.

We all know that over the years wedding styles and even ceremonies have changed. Today, many couples like to personalize their wedding by writing their own vows. They want to express their own ideas about love, God, and their relationship to one another, while keeping the traditional religious aspect of the wedding ceremony. Since much time and personal thought goes into this effort, some couples are having wedding booklets printed to share as souvenirs with their guests.

There are brides and grooms who compose their own words and music for guitar, while some choose contemporary songs to be sung, and others cling to traditional classical wedding music. Some couples carefully select appropriate poems to be read during the ceremony. A few artistic couples design their own creative invitations or original wedding cake. Weddings are readily adapting to our current attitudes and lifestyles, and we expect they will continue to do so in the future.

The one thing that never changes is peoples' tender feelings. When planning a wedding there are so many people on both sides of the family who are emotionally involved, it is wise to consider their sensitivities, to put yourself in their shoes. True, every couple contemplating marriage is deeply involved in their own intense feelings and rightly so! Yet, to prevent any misunderstandings, some guidelines have been developed that are not designed to plague us but rather to relieve us and help make our job smoother and less complicated. If at any time these guidelines interfere with our ability to be kind, thoughtful, and considerate, they should be modified to accommodate the present situation.

Wouldn't it be wonderful if everyone could readily understand how we arrived at our decisions! Unfortunately this is not always so. Customs vary in different parts of the country. A seven o'clock wedding may be a very chic time to have a candlelight service in Washington, D.C., and it may be a most practical time among dairy farmers who are through milking at dusk. There are also great contrasts in some religious and ethnic groups. What one group takes for granted, another group may find quite strange. It is hoped that both families graciously accept differences in ceremonial and social customs as they arise.

Sometimes there are three or four generations involved in a wedding, and it may be difficult for the older generation to adapt to new and different ways of doing things. When the younger generation wishes to be innovative, they may need to consider and respect the feelings of kindly relatives and be open to compromise on unimportant details.

For all the above reasons, it is recommended that friendly communication be developed early on between the families of the bride and groom. This is especially true when either stepparents or stepchildren are involved. Thorny etiquette questions may arise that can test the wisdom of Solomon. During a particularly touchy period in a friend's life, I was asked, "How far does one go?" And my answer was, "All the way!" To go not halfway but all the way in meeting a new situation may be the most fruitful decision a couple can make together.

To guarantee that this experience will be joyful and uplifting, do accept any help that is offered by family and friends. It takes teamwork to orchestrate the numerous details. If someone says, "What can I do to help?" be prepared and tell them! If a friend has lovely handwriting, you may ask for help in addressing envelopes for the invitations and/or announcements. If a neighbor is skilled at arranging flowers, ask if she'll help on the day of the reception. If you need someone to provide transportation for out-of-town guests, let a family member play the role of chauffeur. Everyone enjoys being caught up in the excitement of a wedding.

And going one step further, a positive way to include those special members of the family is to assign honor roles to a favorite aunt, stepparent, grandfather and/or cousin by saying, "Will you do us the honor of recording gifts at our reception?" Not only will these people feel flattered by your request, but they will usually do a most responsible and helpful job at the reception. These assignments will also free the attendants of the wedding party to enjoy themselves more at the reception. Any of the following duties are suitable for your consideration:

Someone to receive and record gifts at the reception.

Someone to supervise the signing of the guest book.

Someone to serve or supervise the punch or refreshment table.

Someone to serve or supervise the cutting of the wedding cake.

Someone to mingle and introduce guests.

Someone to assist the photographer in identifying special guests.

Someone to act as master of ceremonies on the dance floor.

Besides the aforementioned changes in styles of wedding services, in family mores, and in other cross-cultural attitudes, we need to define clearly and precisely the meaning of words in order to avoid misunderstandings. I'm thinking of words pertaining to dress, such as casual, informal, semiformal, and formal. Nowhere is there more confusion in all parts of the country and all segments of society! And nowhere is there a greater pitfall when trying to communicate by telephone with family members who live in various sections of the country about what to wear to a wedding.

Here's a typical story, though a bit extreme, to illustrate the point. A couple visiting in another city were invited to a wedding. They called to ask what to wear and were told the wedding was "informal." At the proper time the couple arrived—the man wearing a blue suit, white shirt, and striped tie only to find, much to their chagrin, that everyone else was dressed in tuxedos! The dinner jacket is considered "informal" in this group as opposed to the cutaway suit with white tie, which is considered "formal."

The word casual can mean anything from tennis shoes and a parka among the young to Gucci loafers and a camel-hair sports coat without a tie among an older group. For our purposes then, when referring to wedding attire in this book, the word casual is omitted entirely. Informal for men means a suit and tie; for women it means a dress. Semi-formal is another grey area that can mean a dark suit (except in the summer in warm climates) or a tuxedo for men and a dressy cocktail dress for the women. Formal may mean a black or white tie for the men and a long or short cocktail gown for the women. The only way to know for sure is to pin people down and find out exactly what they are wearing at that time of the year in their section of the country, at a specified hour of the day.

What the bride and groom decide to wear is discussed in detail in a later chapter. There's just one more factor that bears mentioning and that is that a couple should be dressed in harmony. In other words, if the bride wishes to wear a formal gown with a long train, she must be sure the groom is willing to dress his part as well. The same holds true for the groomsmen. If there is a financial problem, this should be discussed openly and either resolved by the bride and groom, who may offer to subsidize the rental of a suit, or the attendant may graciously decline the honor of serving in the bridal party. All matters of budget are discussed in detail in the third chapter.

CHAPTER 2

The Engagement, Showers, and Prewedding Parties

There is no remedy for love than to love more.

HENRY DAVID THOREAU

It's wonderful to be engaged! A young couple may have mixed feelings—one minute they want to keep this delicious secret to themselves, and the next minute they want everyone to know!

Most parents probably won't be surprised to hear the good news, because chances are they are well aware of this flowering relationship. It is still a courtesy, however, for the young man and woman to have that "special" talk with mother and father.

The ideal length for an engagement, if one is planning a traditional wedding, is from four to six months, as it takes that much time to comfortably make all the necessary arrangements. For an informal home or garden wedding and reception, three months or less, depending on the circumstances, will do nicely.

Couples who intend to get married in the very immediate future or who have been living together for some time or who are marrying for the second time may prefer to forego the formalities of newspaper engagement announcements and parties. Instead, they will announce the wedding date to their family and friends at an informal gathering.

Once a couple is engaged, the man is referred to as the fiancé (a word borrowed from the French), and the woman is called the fiancée. Both words are pronounced the same way: fee-ahn-say. "May I introduce you to my fiancé?" clearly means the couple is formally engaged and a public announcement has been made to friends and relatives.

ANNOUNCING THE ENGAGEMENT
TO THE FAMILY

After parents, the first people to tell of your engagement are close relatives and friends. If possible, make the announcement at any family gathering where everyone can hear the good news at the same time and share your happiness. Before planning a newspaper release, it is considerate to write a note or telephone grandparents, aunts, uncles, and old friends on both sides of the families. It is especially considerate to call on elderly or invalided members of the family. Everyone is interested in a wedding and would like to hear it first from you!

If you haven't met your fiancé's parents, or he hasn't met yours—now is the time. The next step is to have both sets of parents meet or write each other. It is customary and friendly, but not mandatory, for the bridegroom's parents to contact the bride's parents and welcome their daughter as a member of the family. I feel one should not stand on ceremony, and the sooner communication is opened up between both sets of parents the better! It may take time for both sets of parents to get accustomed to the idea, so you may need to exercise a little patience before you begin discussing wedding plans or setting a date.

THE ENGAGEMENT RING

When selecting engagement and wedding rings, keep your budget firmly in mind. There's no need to feel pressured to buy an engagement ring right now. It's possible to combine the engagement and wedding ring, as many do, in one wide band that is inset with small diamonds or any other stone.

Some couples put off getting an engagement ring for years until a special anniversary. This gift can be just as meaningful then as now—perhaps more so.

Although the diamond is usually considered traditional for an engagement ring, any stone, such as the bride or groom's birthstone, is appropriate. An antique ring or treasured family heirloom may be handed down to the bride, or if she has a ring or stone in her family, it is quite proper for the groom to have it reset at his own expense and present it to her.

Quite often, jewelers sell the engagement and wedding ring in a set made of the same material because the two rings fit comfortably on one finger. The bride should be sure to try both rings on and see how they look and feel on her hand before making her selection.

Rings for a Second Marriage

What does the bride do with her first engagement and wedding ring? If there are children from a former marriage, these rings are usually kept for them. Otherwise the first engagement ring may be reset in a new design and worn as a dinner ring.

Engraving

The wedding band is usually engraved on the inside, although the engagement ring is not. About a month or more before the wedding, arrangements should be made to have the ring engraved. Usual inscriptions on the bride's ring are the groom's initials first, the bride's initials, and the date.

If the band is wide enough, there may be room for a brief appropriate sentiment.

The groom's wedding band, if engraved, has the bride's initials first, then his initials, and the date. If she wishes, any meaningful phrase may also be included.

When looking for a reliable jeweler, try to deal with one who is a certified gemologist with a certificate from the Gemological Institute of America. This is the leading authority on diamonds in America. Jewelry stores that have been in business for many years have trained staff to help you make a sound choice. They will explain the differences in carat weight, clarity, color and cut, which determines the price of each stone. (These factors are known as the Four C's.) In addition, you will be supplied with an appraisal certifying the quality for insurance purposes.

Insurance

If the ring is particularly valuble, it's a good idea to have it insured. Many insurance companies don't like to insure expensive rings and will do so only if it is part of a household or other insurance. Some companies are known to include clauses in small print that disclaim responsibility for items such as engagement rings. Some insurance companies will only replace a lost or stolen ring at the appraisal value, which may in time be a lot less than its replacement value. Another common loophole is for the company to insure the entire ring if it is lost, but if only the stone is lost, the company is not liable! Read the fine print carefully, and if it's not possible to get the coverage needed, go to another firm. An added protection is to take a good close-up photograph of your ring with a description and specify on the back of the picture the cut, carats, and color of the diamond to be insured.

Birthstones

January	Garnet or Zircon
February	Amethyst
March	Aquamarine or Bloodstone
April	Diamond
May	Emerald
June	Pearl
July	Ruby
August	Sardonyx or Peridot
September	Sapphire
October	Opal or Moonstone
November	Topaz
December	Turquoise or Lapis Lazuli

ENGAGEMENT PARTIES

*Where there's room in the heart
there is room in the house.*

DANISH PROVERB

Most families become very enthusiastic at the prospect of a wedding, and the bride's parents or a relative may wish to announce the engagement officially at a luncheon, tea, cocktail buffet, or sit-down dinner. This party may take place in the home, at a private club, or in a restaurant—but not in a nightclub! There usually is an element of surprise and no mention is made of the forthcoming announcement on the invitation. After all the guests are assembled, the bride's father or close relative makes the engagement announcement by standing and proposing a toast to the future bride

19

and groom: "Will you all join me in a toast to my daughter, Jennifer, and to the newest member of our family—Bob." The groom then stands and responds with a toast to the bride and her parents by saying something like this: "I don't have to tell you how lucky I am! Jennifer and I want to thank you all for being here and for your good wishes."

If the bride's parents live too far away, there is no reason why the fiancé's parents cannot give the engagement party. When both sets of parents live in the same city, they may choose to cohost a party. Or the couple themselves may plan a small, informal gathering to introduce friends and relatives to each other.

There are innumerable ways of breaking the news at the party, and your own good taste and imagination may provide many novel or interesting ideas. Cocktail napkins, a cake or mints with the couple's names or photographs are but a few suggestions.

SECOND MARRIAGE

Before a couple announce their engagement publicly, it is a courtesy for widows and widowers to inform their former in-laws, preferably by letter. It's wiser to write a short note than to telephone because it may be difficult for former in-laws to handle the unexpected news gracefully. Whereas, given a little time, they may share the news of a second marriage with their genuine blessing. They may be invited to the wedding but do not sit in the reserved section.

When there is an amicable divorce, the same courtesy holds true, especially where children are involved. The former spouse, as well as the grandparents, are informed of the new circumstances, but they are not invited to the wedding.

NEWSPAPER ANNOUNCEMENT AND PHOTOS

A newspaper announcement is easy to prepare. Many papers have forms to be filled out, or you may type the copy, double-spaced on 8½-by-11-inch white bond paper. In the upper right-hand corner list the name, address, and telephone number of the person the newspaper is to contact for additional information. In the upper left-hand corner type the words, "FOR IMMEDIATE RELEASE", or give a definite release date.

Immediately below this line, type a brief headline that tells the editor at a glance what the story is about. For example: "Jennifer Lovejoy engaged to Robert Baldwin."

The newspaper announcement should read more or less like this:

> Mr. and Mrs. Loren Jay Lovejoy of Harbor Springs announce the engagement of their daughter, Jennifer, to Mr. [optional] Robert William Baldwin, son of Dr. and Mrs. Curtis William Baldwin of Lake Forest, Illinois.

If the bride's parents are divorced, either parent may announce the engagement, but the father *must* be mentioned in the story. When a parent or parents are deceased, the engagement may be announced by a close relative, guardian, or friend. The word "late" should then precede any reference made to either of the parents. If the mother is deceased and the father has remarried, the announcement could also read as follows:

> Mr. and Mrs. Roger Smith of Mt. Vernon, New York, announce the engagement of Mr. Smith's daughter, Diane Alice, to Bruce George Compton.

21

Or it is quite proper for a woman to announce her engagement herself as follows:

> Miss Alyce Rogers has announced her engagement to Mr. Hans William Bennett.

If a woman has been married before, she may use either her maiden name or previous married name, whichever is better known to her friends. When the woman has a medical title it is abbreviated, Dr. Margot Smith, and it may be used in newspaper announcements only if the bride announces her own engagement. If her parents issue the announcement, her title is not used, for instance: "their daughter, Margot Smith." When her profession is mentioned later, she is referred to as Dr. Smith.

The second paragraph lists more information about the bride—her school, clubs, sorority, and other affiliations and, if she is employed, the name of the firm (optional).

The third paragraph gives information about the groom. It names his parents and where they live. If the groom's parents are divorced it says:

> Mr. Bruce George Compton is the son of Mrs. Robert MacArthur of Berkeley, California, and Mr. Carl Compton of Anaheim, California.

The groom's schools and possibly his job title and the name of his company are mentioned, as well as any past military rank or branch of the service in which he has served. The names of clubs, fraternities, and other affiliations are also listed.

The fourth paragraph could mention the names of grandparents, especially if they are well known. It is not, however, in good taste to list all the parents' or grandparents' achievements in such a way as to detract from the engagement announcement. The following comments are sufficient, for example:

> The grandparents of the prospective bridegroom reside in Washington, D.C., where Judge Compton is a member of the Supreme Court.

The final paragraph can mention the couple's future plans either in a general way: "The couple plan a spring wedding," or the date and place of the wedding may be included.

Photographs

Sometimes newspapers print the photograph of the prospective bride. It's a good idea to check first with the local paper. Or submit an 8½-by-10-inch glossy print with the name and address taped to the back of the photo with the request, "Please return!" With luck, the picture will be returned, or it may be picked up at the newspaper office. A statement, "Miss Jennifer Lovejoy whose engagement to Mr. Robert Baldwin is announced," should be attached.

Usually, only the photo of the prospective bride is submitted, but this is changing. A picture of the couple may be used as well.

WHEN ENGAGEMENTS ARE ENDED

Ending an engagement is always unpleasant, but the sooner this is faced squarely the better. Remember, *no explanations are necessary!*

The ring and any gifts are, of course, returned immediately to family and friends.

An announcement in the newspapers is optional. Some people feel it's easier on everyone if a release is sent to the paper as follows:

> Mr. and Mrs. Lloyd Jones of Franklin Village announce that the engagement of their daughter Maria has ended by mutual consent.

Be sure, however, not to act hastily before submitting such a release. Lovers quarrel and they also make up!

JOINT CHECKING ACCOUNT

In some cases an engaged couple may wish to open a joint checking account or joint savings account to cover expenses for the wedding reception, honeymoon, etc. Be aware that complications can arise as in the case of a broken engagement, when it is difficult to return gifts of money that have been spent on household furnishings and so forth. It is better to leave the money intact, in the bank. This sum can be spent after the wedding.

BRIDAL SHOWERS AND PREWEDDING PARTIES

The lasting benefit resulting from meeting people at prewedding events is that both sides of the family and their friends become acquainted, possibly for the first time, and grow to know and like each other. Then, by the time the wedding day arrives, everyone feels more relaxed, and the reception is not a stiff, up-tight affair, but one that's jolly with a lively spirit of warmth, congeniality, and friendliness.

Who Gives a Shower?

This question is often asked. Any close friend, neighbor, aunt, cousin, or member of the bridal party may offer to give a shower. Members of the immediate family such as a mother, sister, or grandmother should not act as hostess, although they may share the facilities of their home or give some financial aid.

Showers are usually given a month or more before the wedding, and it's a good idea for two or three people to join forces rather than have too many showers, which can become a financial drain on guests who are invited to four or five showers for the same person. One or two showers is a sensible limit, and each shower can be planned for a different group. Fifteen people, more or less, is a reasonable number for a home shower.

Who Is Invited?

The hostess usually consults with the bride, and perhaps the groom too, regarding the guest list. There is no rule saying that only people who are invited to the wedding may be invited to a shower or the other way around. Much depends on where the wedding is to take place, the size of the wedding, and the size of the reception. For example, one shower might include people from school, club, or office, and it is perfectly all right for the hostess to limit the guest list to only members of this group. Another shower might include relatives and friends of the family, along with the bridesmaids, matron of honor, the flower girl and her mother; or a his-and-her shower would include the ushers, best man, and fathers of the bride and groom. More about these later.

Planning a Shower

The hostess and the bride select a date that is mutually convenient, and they decide what kind of a shower is the most appealing—kitchen, linen, miscellaneous. The hostess may even hint to the guests on written invitations as to the couple's choice of decor—contemporary, provincial, "crafty," along with color preferences.

The Bride's Responsibility

As guest of honor she will try to be considerate and help the hostess in any way she can ahead of time. She will arrive about half an hour early to offer help with last-minute preparations. She will assist by greeting and introducing guests to one another. She will thank each person for her gift and write thank-you notes to those people who sent gifts but were unable to attend the shower.

The Game Plan

A brief game or two always generates lively conversation, fun and laughter. Any paper-and-pencil game, guessing game, or party game helps to break the ice and allows people to know each other better. After the game, refreshments are served, and then the high point of the shower is always at the end with the opening of the brightly wrapped gifts and the reading of the names from the enclosed cards.

The His and Her Shower

Several couples may enjoy splitting the cost and doubling the fun for a "His and Her" shower. Such showers and prewedding events are growing more and more popular in

every community. Among the invited guests are the bridesmaids, the matron of honor, ushers, the best man, and
friends. Any type of party may be planned to suit the locale
and the season ranging from an informal cookout to a
glamorous cocktail party; a charming brunch or a beautiful
buffet supper.

An informal invitation reads as follows:

> *Janet and Bob Linney*
> *Larry and Maryellen Smith*
> *invite you to attend a shower*
> *in honor of*
> *Jennifer Lovejoy and Bob Baldwin*
> *Sunday, May tenth at five o'clock*
> *510 Oakwood Avenue*

RSVP   Kitchen Shower
347-6443

Be sure to give the last names of all persons involved as
there are too many "Janet and Bob," "Mary and Bill" invitations that are puzzling and difficult to link to the people you
know through school, church, or work. It's especially important to give full names if guests are invited because they
are friends of the bride and groom and have never met the
hosts!

Suggested shower themes for a couple's shower are a
kitchen/bar shower or a household accessory/garden shower
or a paper/barbecue shower.

A Bridesmaids Party

The bride may wish to give a party in honor of her bridesmaids and matron of honor prior to the wedding. Both
mothers are included and perhaps the flower girl and her

mother, too. This is a good opportunity to give the attendants their special gifts. It's best to let the bridesmaids know if such a party is in the offing, because a competing surprise party may be planned by all the attendants. They in turn may present the bride with a special gift at this time.

The Bachelor Party

The bachelor party may be sponsored by the groom, his father, best man, or all the ushers. Plans pertaining to the stag affair are usually kept secret. It is a good opportunity for the groom to give them their gifts at this time. The traditional toast to the bride may start or close the festivities.

The bachelor party should be held several days before the wedding so that it will not interfere with the rehearsal dinner. In some cases, bridesmaids and bachelor parties are scheduled for the same day, and the two groups join afterwards. In general, bachelor parties are not held as often as they used to be, especially when ushers come from far away and frequently arrive just in time for the rehearsal the day before the wedding.

The Rehearsal Dinner

It is becoming more and more popular for the wedding rehearsal to be held in the late afternoon the day before the wedding, followed by a rehearsal dinner. Often the groom's parents or relatives enjoy hosting this event because it draws them a little closer into the wedding circle. However, any close friend or relative of either family may opt for this honor. Often the rehearsal dinner is a jolly, informal, stand-up buffet with a relaxed and undressy atmosphere. Or it may be a sit-down dinner at home or at a club or restaurant with placecards. Guests at the rehearsal dinner include all members of the wedding party, both sets of parents, the clergyman or judge and his wife. The spouses and fiancées of married members of the bridal party should be included. Unless there is something else planned for out-of-town guests, it is considerate to include them, too.

At this time the bride and groom may give the attendants their presents if they have not already done so. This is also a good time to sign the marriage license, which is then given to the best man for safekeeping until just before the ceremony, at which time it is presented to the clergyperson or judge.

Family Receptions before or after the Wedding

A reception or dinner may be given either before or after the wedding by either set of parents to introduce the bride and groom to friends and relatives. This is often the ideal solution when the couple is married a great distance from the bride or groom's hometown. Such an invitation may read as follows:

BEFORE THE WEDDING

Mr. and Mrs. Lawrence Franklin
request the pleasure of your company
at a reception
in honor of
Miss Julie Franklin
and
Mr. Thomas Morris
Sunday, the sixteenth of May
from five to seven o'clock
Lord John's Inn
Highland Park, Illinois

Please respond
510 Liberty Street
Oak Park, Illinois 60011

AFTER THE WEDDING

Mr. and Mrs. Joshua Petrillo
request the pleasure of your company
at a dinner
in honor of the marriage of
Mr. and Mrs. Ricardo Onorato
on
Saturday, the fifteenth of May
at half after seven o'clock
Old Orchard Road
Rochester, New York

A response card with stamped envelope may be included.

Parties for Out-of-Town Guests

When there are a number of out-of-town guests, and especially if people are coming from a great distance, it's thoughtful to offer a little extra hospitality. And here's where friends of the family can help. Willing friends can take the guests on sightseeing trips or entertain them at an informal gathering. A generous offer of this kind is always deeply appreciated, particularly the day before the wedding when the bridal party is involved with the rehearsal dinner.

On the day of the wedding, if the ceremony is scheduled late in the day, it is tremendously helpful when a friend or relative offers to give a casual, light luncheon for the bridal party and out-of-town guests. The luncheon should be brief and informal allowing the guests to leave in plenty of time to get dressed for the wedding.

Prewedding party suggestions are listed here, beginning with a morning coffee or brunch and continuing through the day and evening.

The more, the merrier; the fewer, the better fare.

PROVERB

Morning Coffee

The Place: In the garden using coordinated paper goods; or in winter climates, a very posh setting in front of the grate fire using your finest china. The Menu: Serve Bloody Marys, iced tea, or hot chocolate with whipped cream, along with coffee cake, sweet rolls on trays with lacey paper doilies and sliced fresh fruit in a lovely glass bowl or on a platter.

Brunch

The Place: A poolside brunch on a sunny weekend for couples may be as casual as a keg of beer or as elegant as bubbly champagne. The Informal Menu: Indoors or out, a brunch between twelve and two o'clock usually consists of fruit, sweet rolls, a casserole of scrambled eggs with bacon and/or sausages. Champagne Brunch Menu: Halved grapefruit, Eggs Benedict, dessert with coffee.

Luncheon

The Place: At home, a buffet luncheon may be served on a patio outside; indoors, it may take place at a sit-down luncheon or in a Country Club setting or in a lovely private dining room of a restaurant with a view. The Menu: A glass of sherry, Dubonnet, or Daiquiris may precede the meal, followed by a chilled salad with dainty sandwiches, a glass of iced tea and dessert. Optional: An ethnic Mexican, Greek, or Chinese meal including a hot dish, salad, dessert, and beverage. Or curried chicken with rice and condiments. Beer goes well with curry.

Tea

Around the world from England to Japan, an afternoon tea is held in the highest esteem. A "little" tea after two o'clock and before five o'clock in the afternoon at home for fifteen or twenty can be as charming as a large, elegant tea for 100 in a garden or country club. A tea dance with music periodically returns to popularity and is an amusing change of pace. The menu always consists of a variety of sweets, dainty sandwiches, fresh fruits, mints, and nuts. Optional: A bowl of alcoholic punch.

Champagne Tea

In a large silver punch bowl, which may be rented, serve champagne punch, along with refreshments.

Silver Champagne Punch: three magnums domestic champagne, one quart Courvoisier (brandy) and several dashes of bitters. Pour over molded ice ring and serve in silver punch bowl. Makes fifty servings of three ounces each.

Cocktails

In any cozy setting, a theme cocktail party with light or heavy hors d'ouevres is a delightful way to entertain. Especially if you serve a drink specialty such as Southern Mint Juleps, Mexican Margueritas, a nautical Hot Grog, or a punch bowl filled with the typical English drink, Whiskey Sour.

Dessert Party

A good time to entertain: 7:30 P.M. for women or couples. The menu usually consists of a variety of eye-appealing desserts; cakes, trifle or tortes; pies or pastries. For something a little unusual, Cafe Brûlot, Flaming Crêpes or Cherries Jubilee add pizazz to any gathering.

Dinners

Informal cookouts at home with shish-kebob, chicken, or a fabulous hearty soup served in a classic tureen, with a wonderful salad and good, homemade bread can spark a memorable evening. Or you may plan to dine out at a sit-down dinner in the private dining room of a popular restaurant. Here a preplanned menu is desirable to insure better service. You can order flowers for the table ahead of time and prepare small bowls of mints and nuts as well as placecards to make the dinner appear more intimate and private. It is important to know exactly how many people will be present, so if everyone has not RSVP'd the written invitation, it will be wise to telephone and inquire why there's been no response. Mail does go astray and people do leave town, so there's no harm in a follow-up telephone call, if necessary.

CHAPTER 3

---

*The Wedding
Budget*

Spend more imagination than money.

LYNDON B. JOHNSON

Fortunately, the success of a wedding does not depend on a limitless budget. Instead, it is the careful, thoughtful organization that creates the atmosphere on a perfect wedding day.

Every couple needs to determine their own priorities. For example, a daytime wedding followed by a stand-up reception is far less costly than a candlelight wedding followed by a sit-down dinner. To compromise a bit here and there may be better now than to lunge ahead into a nightmare of impractical plans that must be scrapped or, worse, to assume burdensome debts later.

There was a time when wedding expenses were clearly defined and everyone knew who was responsible for what. Parents of the young bride hosted the wedding and paid all the bills. The groom or his parents paid for the honeymoon, and so on. Today these lines are blurred. Families are more flexible. More often than not, the groom's parents make a contribution toward wedding expenses or host the wedding. More couples today are hosting their own wedding completely. In some cases the bride's parents may clearly state the amount they are willing to spend, and anything beyond this sum may be picked up by the bride, the groom, or his parents.

A good time to discuss the budget is when the invitation list is put together, if not before. The wording on invitations and announcements often depends on who is hosting the wedding or who is paying the bills.

For example, if the parents of the bride are giving the wedding, then the invitations are sent out in their name:

Mr. and Mrs. Loren Jay Lovejoy
request the honour of your presence
at the marriage of their daughter, etc.

If, on the other hand, a couple host their own wedding, the invitation may read:

The honour of your presence is requested
at the marriage of
Miss Jennifer Anne Lovejoy
and
Mr. Robert William Baldwin, etc.

(Please refer to Chapter 6—Announcements, Invitations, Stationery.)

In today's unpredictable economy, it is difficult to give prices in anything but general terms. A good rule of thumb for a simple informal wedding today is usually less than two thousand dollars. The cost of a moderate or semiformal wedding averages less than five thousand dollars, and the cost of a large, formal wedding is unlimited. Figuring in terms of percentages, wedding costs for 100 guests are as follows: 5 percent stationery; 10 percent photography; 25 percent clothing and gifts; 10 percent ceremony; 40 percent reception, including flowers and music; 10 percent miscellaneous. When there are more guests the reception percentage rises, and the other percentages drop accordingly.

These monetary figures can be sliced when friends offer innovations that help to set a wedding apart. For instance, one couple borrowed an antique car for the ride from the church to the reception. No limousine fee! Another couple accepted a relative's offer to have the reception in her garden. No rental hall expense! And then there was the bride who accepted a friend's offer to design her wedding gown. A big saving!

A word of caution. Never depend solely on a friend for free photographs. This subject is discussed in greater detail in the chapter on photographs.

For your convenience, a summary of items that fall under the wedding budget is listed below with the traditional division of basic wedding expenses. Each family's circumstances are not the same and this will affect your decisions.

THE BRIDE AND HER FAMILY

Bride's wedding dress and accessories
Bride's presents for her attendants
Bride's honeymoon trousseau
Groom's wedding ring if it is a double-ring ceremony
Printed invitations and announcements
Formal wedding photographs, movies, and/or candid pictures
Floral decorations at ceremony and reception
Rental of awnings, tents, or carpet for aisle
Fee for services performed by sexton, organist, or choir
Music for church and reception
Transportation from bride's home to church and reception
All expenses of reception, including rental of hall or club, catering service, food, refreshments, including liquor*, wedding cake, and favors.
Bride's doctor's visit and blood test

---

*In some areas and among certain ethnic groups, the groom traditionally provides the liquor or champagne for the reception. In other circumstances the groom is expected to buy all the flowers for the wedding party.

THE GROOM AND HIS FAMILY

Bride's engagement and wedding rings
Purchase or rental of wedding attire for groom
Groom's doctor's visit and blood test
Marriage license
Clergyman's fee or donation
Gifts for the best man and ushers
Boutonnieres for the groom and the ushers
Bride's bouquet when local custom requires it
Bride's going-away corsage
Corsages for members of both families, unless the bride
    chooses to include them in her florist's order
Bachelor dinner—optional
Honeymoon expenses

BRIDESMAIDS' EXPENSES

Purchase of bridesmaids' dresses and all accessories
Transportation to and from location of wedding
An individual gift to the couple
A shower or luncheon for the bride may be shared

USHERS' EXPENSES

Rental of wedding attire
Transportation to and from location of wedding
An individual gift to the couple
A bachelor dinner may be given by the ushers, the best man,
    or the groom's father or relative

GUESTS' EXPENSES

The groom's parents pay their own transportation and
lodging expenses, as do out-of-town guests. The parents of

the bride and the groom may help in securing accommodations at the home of friends for bridesmaids and ushers or may offer to pay any expenses they may wish to assume.

WEDDING COORDINATOR

Finally, a hint to the professional or working couple who are living away from home. When you are pressed for time or not familiar with the community or both, a professional wedding coordinator might be the perfect answer for you. Most large cities have wedding coordinators who are experienced advisors and take the place of the mother-of-the-bride who used to enjoy doing all the leg work and who had all the answers. With 60 percent of married women working, today's mother-of-the-bride is either following her own career or off on a safari. Thus the freelance wedding coordinator fills the gap. She has the necessary connections at her fingertips to help couples find that perfect place for the reception, select a caterer, find the right music and special florist, help with the wording of invitations, and assist in making the arrangements at the church. She will also be at the rehearsal, ceremony, and even make arrangements for the honeymoon, if you like. A good, experienced wedding coordinator will save you a lot of time and will help you budget wisely. She may work for an hourly rate or charge a percentage of the total wedding cost (usually 15 percent). The wedding coordinator brings repeat business to the florists, photographers, caterers, etc. that she deals with, which gives her a lot of clout, and this works to your advantage! She handles the total wedding on your behalf, with your advice and consent, and will make sure everything runs smoothly.

This professional service is not to be confused with the wedding consultant you find in a department store, bridal shop, jewelry store, stationery store, or florist shop. Such in-house consultants are people who work in a store and specialize in helping the bride and groom with their gift selections, without charge.

I would love to play the role of wedding coordinator and be at your wedding, but since this is impossible, I hope you will find all the helpful answers in the following pages of this book and that your wedding will be just as perfect as you have every right to expect.

THE BRIDE AND GROOM'S CALENDAR

SIX OR MORE MONTHS* BEFORE THE WEDDING:

1. Decide on the type of wedding; where it will be held; who is going to officiate; how many guests will be invited.
2. Discuss budget and estimate costs.
3. Shop for engagement and wedding rings.
4. Meet with your clergyman. Set date and time of wedding.
5. Decide who your attendants will be.
6. Compare facilities for rehearsal and reception sites.
7. Compare prices of local caterers, bakers, florists, musicians, photographers. Check into party rental services chairs, tents, glasses, etc.
8. The bride selects her gown and those of her attendants. The groom selects his suit and those of his attendants. The couple helps mothers to blend gowns with each other and the rest of the wedding party.
9. Visit stores and compare furniture, appliances, and accessories. Register for gifts.
10. Meet with insurance agent regarding insurance on ring, wedding gifts, etc.

*Catholic marriages require at least six months notice for prewedding arrangements with the bride's pastor.

TWO TO THREE MONTHS BEFORE THE WEDDING:

11. Shop for invitations, announcements, and thank-you stationery.
12. Check final invitation and announcement list with both families.
13. Address and stamp envelopes.
14. Make hotel reservations and/or visit your travel agent regarding honeymoon trip. If necessary arrange for passports. Check luggage required for honeymoon.
15. Get birth certificates. Get physical, blood test, and inoculations, if necessary.
16. Meet with musicians and go over music for ceremony and reception.
17. Reserve photographer for ceremony and reception. Make appointment for black and white newspaper photo.
18. Confirm flower orders. Decide on rose petals, confetti, rice bags, if permitted.
19. Finalize arrangements for rehearsal dinner and reception site. Check menus with caterer.
20. Order wedding cake. (Groom's cake and almond souvenirs etc., optional.)
21. Check with bridesmaids regarding gown, shoes, etc. Collect measurements from ushers and order rental suits.
22. Select gifts for attendants. (Monogramming optional.)

ONE MONTH BEFORE THE WEDDING:

23. Mail invitations.
24. Arrange for transportation, maps, and lodging for out-of-town members of the wedding party.
25. Attend prewedding parties. Give gifts to bridesmaids and groomsmen.
26. Bride and groom have final fitting on clothes. Break in shoes.
27. Bride and groom sit for wedding portraits and prepare wedding announcement for newspaper.
28. Check on honeymoon tickets and hotel confirmation.

29. Make hair appointments. Bride schedules makeup artist (optional).
30. Decide where bride, groom, and attendants will dress before the wedding.
31. Get marriage license.
32. Move belongings to new home and arrange utilities, telephone, and mail. Put someone in charge to handle gifts at reception.
33. Write thank-you notes.
34. Spend some quiet times together.

ONE WEEK BEFORE THE WEDDING:

35. Attend prewedding parties. (This is a good time to tell relatives and special friends where to sit during the wedding ceremony, unless you have arranged for pew cards.) Visit with out-of-town guests.
36. Confirm number of wedding guests to caterer.
37. Make final check with florist, photographer, musician, baker.
38. Check on final alterations on groomsmen's suits.
39. Pack for honeymoon trip.
40. Write thank-you notes and placecards.
41. Spend a quiet evening with your family.

THE DAY BEFORE THE WEDDING:

42. Pack toiletries. Lay out wedding clothes and going-away outfits. Groom makes out check to clergyman or judge.
43. Attend rehearsal and dinner and go home early.

ON THE DAY OF THE WEDDING:

44. Eat a substantial breakfast.
45. Get dressed for wedding. Attend the ceremony and reception and have a wonderful time! Change into traveling outfit. Thank everyone sincerely! Leave for honeymoon.

AFTER THE WEDDING:

46. Mail wedding announcements. Call home. Write post-cards to friends while on honeymoon.

AFTER THE HONEYMOON:

47. Unpack and get settled. Exchange duplicate gifts. Write thank-you notes. Invite your first guests to dinner!

CHAPTER 4

Planning the Wedding

Hear the mellow wedding bells
Golden bells!
What a world of happiness their harmony
  foretells!
Through the balmy air of night
How they ring out their delight!

EDGAR ALLAN POE

EARLY DECISIONS

Major decisions that influence every detail of the wedding and the budget are as follows. Will it be a religious or civil ceremony? Where will the reception be held? When is the best time to have the wedding? How many guests will be invited? If the groom has been married before, that fact has no effect on the size or elegance of a bride's first wedding.

A RELIGIOUS OR CIVIL CEREMONY

Selecting the clergy member or judge goes hand in hand with selecting the site of the ceremony. If a priest, minister, or rabbi is preferred, the wedding will probably be held in a church, temple, college chapel, the rectory, or the pastor's study. But if a mayor or judge is selected, the ceremony could take place at City Hall or in the judge's chambers. Some rabbis, judges, and Protestant ministers perform wedding ceremonies in a hotel, restaurant, or private club, in a garden, or in the bride's parents' home. Sometimes a friend or relative may offer her home or garden for the wedding. In some communities it's possible to rent a lovely mansion, art center, public park, or historic site for both the wedding and reception.

For a semiformal wedding, almost any good-sized room can be transformed into a churchlike setting. Furniture may be moved or removed as the case may be. Folding chairs are set up in a V formation, which makes it possible for people near the wall to see the altar. Room is left for a center aisle between the rows of chairs. A raised platform may be installed for the ceremony.

No matter where the ceremony takes place—in a church, club, hotel, garden, or in a home—the location may be either in the bride's hometown or the groom's hometown or in the city where the engaged couple presently live and work.

A variety of combinations of ceremonies and reception sites may be considered, but let's limit ourselves first to a few popular sites for the ceremony.

Home Weddings

It is not necessary to try to seat every guest during the ceremony when it is held indoors. Home ceremonies are usually brief, and as long as there is seating for the older generation, others don't mind standing. Just be sure to remove tippy tables and lamps as well as small pieces of furniture to prevent breakage.

Church Weddings

The advantage of a church wedding is that the building will accommodate a large number of people with little expense. Many guests may attend the ceremony, which may be followed by a simple reception at the church.

Rented Site

Any private setting in a club, restaurant, hotel, hall, or facility may be chosen for a large or small group of people. Here charges may vary from two hundred dollars to over one thousand dollars.

Garden Weddings

Outdoor weddings are lovely, if you can depend on the weather. But always have an alternate plan in case of rain. If the budget allows, a good alternative is to rent a tent.

TENTS

The advantage of renting tents is twofold—they create a colorful, festive atmosphere at home and offer complete protection for guests against hot summer sun or drenching rains.

When the wedding ceremony is held at home, a tent may be rented for the ceremony with either full or partial seating accommodations, with a platform area used for the altar. The platform may be later converted into a dance floor.

After the ceremony, guests may return to the house and go through the receiving line. Meanwhile, a quick change-over process is taking place outside. The tent that was originally used for the wedding ceremony is now turned into a dining tent. Tables that were concealed behind shrubs or in a nearby garage are brought in and set up. Chairs that moments before were used at the ceremony are now placed around the tables. By the time guests have gone through the receiving line and enjoyed their first drink, everything is in readiness for the reception.

For a more elaborate arrangement, two tents may be set up, one for the ceremony and one for dinner.

Tents come in all sizes, from 16 by 16 feet, which will seat 25 guests, up to 60 by 90 feet, which will seat over 500 guests. And there are tents that will accommodate as many as 5,000 guests. They can be heated and, in some areas, air conditioned.

Tents may be color coordinated with the wedding scheme. They come in a variety of stripes—red/white, yellow/white, green/white or solid pink or blue, for example.

The tent is usually set up a couple of days in advance, which helps to keep the ground dry under the structure. Tents may be placed in the back or front of the house, over asphalt driveways or patio areas. They may even be erected over swimming pools, so that this focal point may be used effectively for outdoor dancing around the pool.

Companies providing this service are highly specialized, and large tenting companies will supply many states.

SETTING THE DATE

When setting the date for the wedding, several things need to be considered, including the season of the year, the day of the week, and the time of the day.

Naturally, couples leaning toward garden weddings, at least in the northeast, know the winter season is out of the question. Conversely, couples yearning for candlelight ceremonies will not choose summer. Lent is usually not chosen by Christians, at least not for a religious ceremony, though simple marriages with or without a clergyman do take place during these forty days of Penitence. Usually, Christians don't choose Sunday for a wedding nor do religious Jews marry on the Sabbath (Friday sundown to Saturday sundown) or on the High Holy Days.

When making plans for the date of the wedding, bear in mind that the time of day and the day of the week will determine the number of acceptances and regrets. Both afternoon and evening weddings followed by a reception held on Saturday or Sunday are much better attended than those held during the week. During vacation periods and holidays, many people have family conflicts and are unable to attend weddings. For most people, Saturday is the favorite day because it is convenient for guests to attend.

THE TIME OF DAY

Many weddings take place in the afternoon followed by a reception. Evening weddings, with candlelight services, are usually more formal and are followed by either a reception or a dinner and dancing. Popular times of the day vary in different parts of the country.

THE GUEST LIST

The guest list can be as unmanageable as a puppy and can grow just as fast!

When a couple is paying for their own wedding, the guest list will probably include a large percentage of the couple's mutual friends with a sprinkling of close relatives.

When the bride's parents are paying for the wedding, the guest list can turn into a stumbling block if not handled tactfully from the beginning. It is only natural that parents will wish to include more of their close friends, because sharing the pleasure doubles the fun! This group ought to be limited, nevertheless, to people who have known the bride and who are interested in her future. It ought not to include all the parents' friends and acquaintances, as this is not a social party to pay off obligations.

In many ethnic circles, on the other hand, it is customary for parents of the bride to open the wedding celebration to the whole community, with festivities lasting for several days.

In checking over the guest list with her parents, the bride may not be in complete accord, but she ought to compromise with her parents' suggestions, if possible. For example, she may not be aware of the genuine interest that her parents' friends have shown over the years, because she was too young to remember. The same consideration holds true for the groom when consulting with his parents. Fortunately, the final decisions always rest with the bride and groom.

When both sets of parents live in the same community, the guest list is equally divided. When the groom's family lives far away, the bride's parents usually invite more people than the groom's family. If there is a problem, the best way to clarify matters to everyone's satisfaction is to have both families meet and discuss the guest list informally. It is becoming more customary for the groom's parents to offer to share in the expense of the reception, particularly if their guest list is a long one.

If it is not possible for the families to meet, the bride may write as tactfully as she can to the groom's parents and advise them how many guests she is planning to invite. She will ask for a copy of their list as soon as possible and hope they will understand that the number of guests is limited for various good reasons.

Is it necessary to invite all the relatives? Not really. If there has been little or no communication in years and they live far away, there is no need to invite them. Still, it's friendly to send an announcement of the marriage, which does not require a gift in return.

Infants in Church and Children at Receptions

Some people like to bring small children to church weddings, and it can be a thrilling and memorable experience for these little folk. However, infants are uncontrollable and unpredictable and may start to cry at the most tender moment of the ceremony. It's not always possible to depend on word of mouth to get the message across that infants should remain at home. Therefore, the farsighted bride might arrange for infants to be taken to the nursery that many churches provide.

If a formal sit-down dinner is planned after the wedding, it may be necessary to restrict the number of children attending the reception, especially if this is a large family with dozens of cousins, nieces, and nephews. It can be done if youngsters are limited to those over a certain age, with no exceptions. Close friends and relatives can help spread the word, or it may be stated on the reception card, "adults only."

Special Guests

This includes people employed in the home: baby sitters, housekeepers, caretakers, and others who are devoted to the family. It's nice to invite a special teacher, a friend's older brother, or someone who has touched your life in a special way. Also send invitations to people who live far away, if you have a warm feeling toward them, as they will be thrilled to know that you have remembered them.

You may wish to invite the parents of your bridesmaids and ushers, if you know them well, but this is optional.

Handicapped Persons

If there is a person in a wheelchair in the wedding party or among the guests, it is necessary to take this into consideration when selecting a site. Arrangements can be made for a portable ramp at the entranceway. Ramps may be rented from a truck rental firm. Bathroom facilities need to be checked as well.

Cancellations

Much as everyone loves weddings, unforeseen circumstances arise that prevent everyone from attending, so be sure to take this into consideration. The number of wedding guests will grow smaller as the day approaches because of these unfortunate last-minute cancellations. Some people estimate the number can reach 25 percent. It's important to estimate carefully how many people will actually attend, because this affects the cost. The caterer or person in charge of handling the reception is experienced in allowing for last-minute regrets; however, he must be advised by a certain date, or the host is billed for every guest, whether he was there or not.

The Final Guest List

The final list of names will be compiled from both sides of the family and from the bride and groom's own friends. After checking for duplications and making sure that no one has been overlooked, you are ready to order your invitations and announcements.

FILE CARDS

A time-saving plan is to take the final guest list and transfer it to file cards. On each card, list the name, address, and phone number of the guest and indicate acceptances or regrets. Also note any gifts received for both shower and wedding and check if these have been acknowledged. Both the bride and groom will find this filing system handy for future reference.

CHAPTER 5

Planning the Reception

Music I heard with you was more than music
And bread I broke with you was more than bread.

MUSIC I HEARD WITH YOU

Because the reception expenses cover such a large percentage of the total budget, planning for a reception is discussed now in this book in detail. What takes place at the reception will be discussed later on (for example, who stands in the receiving line, how to cut the cake, and so forth).

Few people have an unlimited budget at their disposal, so it takes a bit of juggling to decide early on what is important to you and what is not. Since everyone is invited to the reception, now is the time to settle on the size and place so that there will be sufficient funds allocated to cover the additional wedding expenses for music, flowers, gifts, photographs, etc.

WHEN THERE IS NO RECEPTION

At a small church wedding, when there is no reception, the bride and groom with their attendants and family may greet their guests informally in the vestibule of the church or any pleasant spot near the exit.

RECEPTIONS IN CHURCH AND TEMPLE

Many churches and temples have a social room available for wedding receptions after the ceremony, for which a small fee is charged. Most churches do not allow any wine or alcoholic beverages to be served, although they may be served in temple. Some congregations provide all accessories: tablecloths, silver, china, and may even suggest the name of a caterer. In church, the menu usually consists of a nonalcoholic fruit punch and soft drinks, with small sandwiches and cake. If the church has a lawn or a garden, the doors may be opened, and the guests may stroll outside if the weather allows. A piano or guitar player are bound to add gaiety and sparkle to the occasion.

PRIVATE RECEPTIONS

The reception may be held immediately after the ceremony in a home, restaurant, or club. The bride's parents' house is a favorite and traditional setting for a wedding reception. Refreshments may be served at a stand-up buffet table (indoors), or during warm weather, if the house is too small to seat all the guests, a tent may be set up in the garden and the house may be used as a place for depositing coats and for providing bathroom facilities for the guests; rooms for the bride, groom, and attendants to dress; and a kitchen for the catering staff.

It's a relief to know that at a short reception it is not necessary to provide chairs for everyone because it's fun for guests to walk about and mingle. Usually some chairs and tables are provided for older friends and relatives. When there is dancing, café chairs and tables may be used.

INFORMAL HOME RECEPTIONS

In some cases, friends and relatives may offer to prepare refreshments, help serve and clean up. Decide in advance what you are going to serve, when it will be served, and select platters, bowls, china, flatware, napkins, and glasses along with serving utensils, flower holders, and candlesticks. Tape a small piece of paper for handy reference to each bowl and platter with the label written clearly—*fruit bowl, cheese platter; sandwiches;* etc., and place the appropriate serving utensil to be used on each platter and in each bowl. You can even make a diagram of the buffet table in advance. Most communities have party rental stores where much of the above-mentioned equipment may be rented. The advantage here is that the buffet table has an attractive, uniform appearance, instead of giving a pot-luck-supper impression.

To be sure that everything will go smoothly, designate someone reliable to be in charge of the kitchen, station another person at the refreshment table to see that platters are kept filled and remain appetizing in appearance, and designate someone to pour the champagne, serve punch, or handle the bar. Remember the bride and groom will both be much too busy having pictures taken, talking to guests, and cutting the wedding cake to supervise the refreshment table.

Setting the Buffet Table

Set the buffet table in logical sequence. The dinner plate comes first; then the hot food—meat (precut), vegetables, potatoes, and casseroles; then cold food such as salads and ring molds. It's convenient for the guests to pick up the flatware and napkin *after* they have helped themselves to the food. Better yet, roll the flatware in a napkin or place it in a pocket napkin fold.

Buffet service or selfservice is when each person helps himself to a plate, food, flatware, and napkin.

Semi-buffet or partial selfservice is when the dining table has been set with flatware, napkins, and glasses, and guests

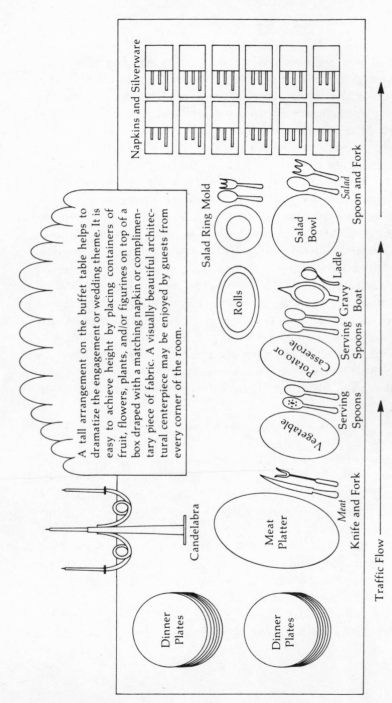

A tall arrangement on the buffet table helps to dramatize the engagement or wedding theme. It is easy to achieve height by placing containers of fruit, flowers, plants, and/or figurines on top of a box draped with a matching napkin or complimentary piece of fabric. A visually beautiful architectural centerpiece may be enjoyed by guests from every corner of the room.

Napkins and Silverware

Salad Ring Mold

Rolls

Salad Spoon and Fork

Salad Bowl

Ladle

Serving Gravy Boat
Spoons

Potato or Casserole

Serving Spoons

Vegetable

Candelabra

Meat Knife and Fork

Meat Platter

Dinner Plates

Dinner Plates

Traffic Flow →

BUFFET SETTING AND CENTER PIECE

merely serve themselves from the buffet and then seat themselves at the tables. When the main course is finished, the table is cleared and dessert is served.

PARTY RENTAL STORES

Party rental stores have mushroomed all over the country. People are depending more and more on this convenient equipment rental service, especially for home or garden weddings.

Most party rental stores supply anything from one dozen glasses to tables, chairs, bars, and tents, and many include table linen, lace skirting for the buffet and cake tables, flatware, chinaware and glassware as well as platters, chafing dishes, pitchers, and bowls. They also carry floral standards and arches for garden weddings, along with portable dance floors and champagne fountains. The latter come with full instructions.

Some party rental stores have several grades of linen, including damask, silver-plated table service, and a nice selection of wine glasses; while others offer only cotton cloths and stainless-steel flatware. Again, it pays to shop around.

To save time and energy, telephone the rental store ahead and ask a few pertinent questions, or have them send you a brochure of available items. Most rental stores pride themselves on giving good service, because word of mouth referral is what keeps them in business. Orders will be delivered in cartons at a predesignated time, and the order must be repacked in cartons ready for pick-up.

To assure first-choice selections, rental supplies must be reserved early, as many people book their orders well in advance.

THE WEDDING CAKE

The highlight of every reception is the charming ritual when the bride cuts the first slice of cake, which she offers to the groom to signify that she is willing to share with him now and forever. A photograph of the bride and groom performing this symbolic bit of domesticity is included in almost every wedding album.

Selecting the right wedding cake means comparing prices and looking at samples of one- to four-tiered decorated cakes from a reliable bakery. Most bakers have pictures and order forms that include all the necessary information describing the cake, the delivery date and time, the address of the reception site, the name of the person who will receive the cake, and the bride's name and phone number in case there is any question. The terms of payment will be included, as well as the amount of the deposit. The baker will keep a copy and give one to the bride for reference.

If the bride and/or groom have the talent and inclination, he or she may undertake baking their own wedding cake. Or perhaps a talented friend, relative, or neighbor has the know-how and experience.

The plus factor when selecting a cake from a professional baker is that he has the facilities to transport a large cake and assemble it at the reception site. In case anything happens to the cake, there is a back-up crew to come to the rescue. The minus factor is that a bakery cake is more expensive.

How big should the cake be? Every pound of cake provides five portions; for 100 people at least a twenty-pound cake is needed.

What flavor? Any flavor—vanilla, lemon, or chocolate, with any kind of filling may be used, but for a very large cake, a pound cake holds up best.

When selecting the decoration for the cake, all white or white with a touch of pastel is really the prettiest and most appetizing. Fresh flowers and leaves are very popular for decorations, as well as dainty decorations made of icing. A natural look is the most favored with leaves tinted green and rosebuds tinted pink or yellow. The buffet table on which the cake is placed may accent the colors used on the cake, which in turn ought to blend with the rest of the color scheme of the reception.

Besides floral decorations, romantic symbols like swans, bells, doves, hearts, or cupids are frequently used to decorate cakes, but it is not usual to put any sort of writing on the cake.

Whether the cake is made at home or in a bakery, top ornaments are very similar. A small nosegay of fresh flowers, such as lilies of the valley, baby orchids or stephanotis can be inserted in a small vial of water at the top of the cake. This keeps the flowers fresh all through the reception. Or it's easy to make orange roses by cutting orange peel with a sharp knife from a large orange in long spirals. The strips are rolled up, orange side out, and fastened with a small pick to the cake. These are placed on the cake at the last minute, just before the guests arrive. The orange roses are garnished with springs of fresh mint or any small, green leaf.

Wedding cakes can be any shape—round, heart-shaped, square, or graduated in tiers. For a military wedding, the cake may be baked in the shape of the bridegroom's corps insignia. (Cutting the cake is described in "On the Day of the Wedding.")

THE GROOM'S CAKE

The groom's cake is usually a dark fruit cake and is not eaten at the reception but taken home by the guests. Originally, the groom's cake was referred to as the wedding cake, and what we think of as wedding cake was called the bride's cake. It is customary, if one cares to follow this tradition, to pack the groom's cake in a small white or silver box, tie it with a ribbon, and place this at each person's place at the table. Or, in the case of a buffet, the boxes are stacked on a tray near the door and every guest takes one on the way home as a memento. The boxes may be printed with the name of the couple and the date. Those who believe in superstition will put the groom's cake under their pillows to dream that night of the person they will marry.

GETTING IT IN WRITING!

When the reception is held in a church or hotel, a restaurant or country club, be sure that the person in charge of arrangements *puts it all in writing!* Too often the person who makes all those lavish promises, is no longer around come the day of your wedding, and the person you are left to deal with chooses not to honor the agreement or surprises you with hidden charges. But when you have all the arrangements in writing on official stationery *with a signature*, there can be no doubts! Here is a brief list of items you want to have in writing.

The Date and Hours

From when to when. Luncheons are usually served between 12:00 and 2:00 P.M., but your guests may choose to linger. Tea receptions are held between 2:00 and 5:00 P.M., and cocktail receptions between 4:00 and 7:30 P.M. A late reception or dinner is served between 7:00 and 9:00 P.M., and this celebration may last until the wee hours, or until the band stops playing. Usually one has a light menu at the earlier hour and a heavier menu for the later hour. Be sure you know when the room will be made available for decorating and when you have to be out. (Your reception might be going full swing when you are unexpectedly asked to leave because the room is reserved for another group!)

The Service

Find out exactly who will be available and how many to do what. Ask about valet parking, coat-room checking, how many waitresses, how many bartenders, and clean-up charges.

The Food

Know what food will be provided and how it will be served. Will platters and chafing dishes be stainless steel, copper, or silver plate? Will platters be garnished? Will paper doilies be used?

The Liquor

Check on the corkage charge. What time will the bar be opened and closed? What kind of glasses are available for champagne or for beer, wine, and punch? Will there be wine bottles at the dinner tables or will it be poured by waiters? What about after-dinner drinks?

The Tables

What kind of tablecloths and napkins are available? Will they be neatly pressed without holes? For a sit-down dinner will there be sufficient flatware: knives, forks, etc. for each course? Will each table be cleared before dessert is served? Will coffee be served with the dessert? (Request that the coffee cups not be on the table at the start of the meal—this looks too much like a coffee shop.)

The Price

Does the price quoted mean per person, and does it include tax and tip? Are there any hidden charges you should know about? Some places charge extra when you bring your own wedding cake. This is called a "service charge" for cutting and serving the cake.

Selecting the Right Room

The size of a room in relation to the number of people is the first consideration. If the room is too large, people feel "lost" in it and don't have much fun. If the room is too small—hot, noisy, and crowded—people will feel equally uncomfortable.

For a daytime reception, select a room with a lovely view or with windows where daylight shines in. For an after-dark reception, select a room that has sparkle, one with mirrors or crystal chandeliers. Have the draperies drawn shut and check to be sure they blend with your color scheme on the tables.

Sometimes a room that looks undesirable in bright daylight can be camouflaged with soft candlelight and flowers in the evening and end up looking most attractive. Or a room that is plain, can be decorated with rented plants and look colorful and charming.

For sit-down lunches or dinners, you will need to check if the room has easy access to the kitchen, which assures you being served a *hot* meal promptly. When you have a band, check for platforms, microphones, and musical outlets.

Finally, know the fire laws regarding the use of candles and flammable materials. (You may need to clear this with the fire department, which will sometimes station a fireman to standby on special occasions.) Fire department codes usually have limits on the number of persons a room can legally hold.

CATERERS

How does one go about finding a caterer? The best way, of course, is to sample the "cates." (Why did such a lovely, solid word ever go out of fashion?) Some caterers serve industry primarily (annual banquets, meetings, and conferences), while others specialize in private functions (weddings, anniversaries, engagements, confirmations, and the like), and some do both.

A caterer may mean anything from a woman who's a fine cook, whose husband happens to own a station wagon, and who will prepare and serve a dinner for sixteen or sixty from your own kitchen; to a large, professional catering service with mobile kitchens, which will either wholly or partially prepare and serve a meal. Some caterers supply everything including fine linens, china, and crystal, while others supply only the food and personnel.

A good caterer will: (1) Welcome your suggestions and help develop your wedding so that it reflects your own taste and personality; (2) Use your own recipes if you wish and keep them confidential; (3) Supply you with bonded, trained waiters, waitresses, and bartenders; (4) Free you from all responsibilities before, during, and after the party.

An experienced caterer will ask for a party-planning conference and confirm all arrangements either in duplicate or triplicate. A conference with a caterer or party consultant should be as honest and aboveboard as any conference between you and your clergyman. Trust his or her judgment, which is based on years of experience. Tell him or her exactly what your budget is, what your facilities are, how many people you plan to invite, and he or she will tell you if it is possible and how it can best be done.

It's a good idea to have a run-through when planning a large party at home. Some hostesses don't realize until the last minute that their kitchen facilities are inadequate, the borrowed pan is too big for the stove, the electrical wiring is inadequate for all the extra cooking equipment plugged in, and so on. Be sure you test the working order of any stored, infrequently used articles such as a fifty-cup coffee maker or folding tables. Then, when the day of the wedding arrives, there won't be any last-minute emergencies. Instead, everything will be just perfect!

ALCOHOLIC AND NONALCOHOLIC BEVERAGES

Since the greatest cost of a reception involves the choice of beverages, I shall go over this subject carefully, item by item. Nonalcoholic beverages, hot or cold, are the least expensive. Served with style, a punch in a crystal or silver punch bowl is a favorite at church receptions where no alcohol is permitted. When allowed, it is thoughtful to offer both alcoholic and nonalcoholic beverages to your guests. A nice way of limiting alcoholic consumption without offense is to serve guests a few drinks and allow them to visit awhile. When it is time for the cake to be cut, fill the champagne glasses for the last time so that everyone may toast the bride. After the bride cuts the first piece of cake, the staff serves each guest a slice along with a cup of coffee. While the guests' attention is thus diverted, no one notices that the bar is being dismantled.

Nonalcoholic Beverages

There are many excellent punch recipes available. We suggest this party punch because it is not too sweet and complements a heavily iced wedding cake. Whenever I have served it, people have begged me for the recipe. It is enjoyed by youngsters and adults alike.

PARTY PUNCH

The tea extract may be prepared days ahead of time and kept in a gallon jug. At serving time, pour tea mixture into punch bowl, then add chilled ginger ale along with frozen chunks of canned pineapple. NO ICE REQUIRED.

TEA EXTRACT:

2 cups boiling water
4 tablespoons tea leaves, black
3 large lemons
2 cups sugar
4 cups cold water
1 teaspoon vanilla extract
1 teaspoon almond extract

SERVING TIME:

2 bottles (28 oz. each) ginger ale, chilled;
1 can pineapple chunks, frozen

TEA EXTRACT: Pour 2 cups of boiling water over tea leaves, not tea bags. Cover and steep for 10 minutes. In the meantime, wash lemons, extract juice, and keep the rinds. Add sugar, water, lemon juice and rinds and heat in a medium-size pan on top of the stove, stirring until sugar is thoroughly dissolved. Strain tea through sieve and add to hot lemon/sugar mixture. When cool, and not before, stir in vanilla and almond extract. Chill until serving time.

BEFORE SERVING TIME: Pour into punch bowl and just before serving, add chilled ginger ale. Float frozen pineapple chunks in punch. Makes 30 cups.

(By permission of Hawaiian Visitors Bureau)

OTHER OPTIONS

One may serve chilled bubbling grape juice that looks and sparkles like champagne in either punch or champagne glasses. Or one may have a tea table, where hot tea and coffee is served. There may be a single or double tea service, one at each end of the table, depending on the number of guests. This requires that a guest of honor be designated to pour and another person delegated to replenish the teapot and coffeepot during the reception.

Alcoholic Punch

A mixed drink, such as Whiskey Sours or Bloody Marys, or a light punch can be mixed and served from a punch bowl or poured from a pitcher. Far less expensive than an open bar, a delicious wine punch is frequently the right answer for an indoor or outdoor reception. (See Silver Champagne Punch in "The Engagement.")

For a summer wedding:

FRESH PEACH PUNCH

3 pounds fresh peaches, sliced
1/4 cup sugar
1/4 cup brandy
1 fifth red wine, chilled
1 fifth white wine, chilled
1 bottle domestic champagne, chilled

Add sugar and brandy to peaches and let stand 3 to 4 hours. Just before serving time, place in crystal punch bowl and pour red and white wine over peaches. Add block of ice, and at the very last minute add champagne.

Makes 24 servings.

Champagne

Here's to champagne the drink divine,
That makes us forget all our troubles;
It's made of two dollars worth of wine
And six dollars worth of bubbles.

Champagne served from the bottle or a punch bowl or a champagne fountain is very elegant. The price varies according to the country of origin. Imported French champagne is considered the finest. However, there are many excellent domestic champagnes on the market. In some communities, a choice of champagne or beer is offered, since the latter is very popular among the young set. However, beer should not be served in a can or bottle but from a keg in glasses. Beer tastes much better out of a glass. (Plastic glasses are only used around pools, where there is a danger of breakage, or under extremely casual circumstances.)

The Open Bar

A great variety of liquor is required to stock an open bar. Fortunately, most liquor-store owners will accept returns of unopened bottles. A brand of scotch, bourbon or rye, gin, vermouth, vodka, and blended whiskey usually suffice. Sherry and white wine are also frequently called for, along with soft drinks. Mixes, such as soda water, quinine water, and ginger ale are needed, as well as lemons, limes, cherries, olives, and cocktail onions. Buckets of cubed and/or crushed ice complete the list. You may instruct the bartender in advance when you want the bar to open and close. He will inform the guests, "The bar is closing in ten (or twenty) minutes."

Tray Service

There are times when it's preferable to have waiters or waitresses pass trays of prepared or mixed drinks. In this case the choices are usually limited. Some drinks are mixed ahead and kept chilled in the refrigerator. When ready to serve, ice and garnishes are added.

How Many Bottles?

No matter how often one entertains, there's always the question, "How many bottles of liquor do we need?" Using the following measurements as a guide, one is able to judge the number of drinks per person. The average guest will have two or three drinks, or figure roughly one drink every half hour per person. A good rule of thumb in gauging how much champagne is required is to figure one bottle for every two people. For a large group and a long reception, it's better to use small glasses (6 oz. or 8 oz.), because people frequently set a glass down and forget where they put it. For this reason, for a long reception with dancing and so forth, you will need about three glasses per person.

1 case of liquor = 12 bottles
1/5 bottle = 1/5 gallon or 7 ounces less than a quart
1/5 bottle liquor, using 1-ounce pony = 25 drinks

1/5 bottle liquor, using 1-1/2-ounce jigger = 18 drinks. (The difference between a pony and a jigger is 1/2 oz.)
1/5 bottle champagne, using 3-ounce glasses = 7 drinks

Step-Savers

When setting up an improvised bar indoors or out, drape a cloth that reaches all the way to the floor around the edge of a large, sturdy table or aluminum folding table. Behind this drape you can store extra liquor, lemons, limes, glasses, soda, empty bottles, and a wastebasket. Keep a large tray handy for quick trips to the kitchen with used glasses.

PLANNING THE ENTIRE MENU

When planning a menu for any occasion, it's been my experience that the easiest way to spark ideas is to jot down food categories on a sheet of paper. For instance, when planning the menu for a reception, the main food categories are: cheese and eggs, fish, fowl, meat, vegetables, fruit, and sweets. By the time you have selected one item from each category, you are already off to a solid menu-planning start. Within each category, consider additional sub-categories such as hot or cold, sweet or sour, or soft or crunchy. For example, it's not a good idea to offer a salad with vinegar dressing when serving wine. And finally, it's important to think of the color in the food itself, such as orange carrots, red beets, black olives, or green melons. If one needs additional color, this may be achieved with garnishings such as green parsley, watercress, mint leaves, sliced cucumbers, or red tomatoes, watermelon, radishes, or cabbage leaves.

Here follow some menu suggestions that may be helpful when planning a wedding reception, brunch, luncheon, buffet, or sit-down dinner. No doubt your final decision will depend on the number of people invited; the season of the year (always taking advantage of fresh fruits and vegetables); the location, if near water where fresh fish or crabmeat is plentiful; the budget, where your imagination counts; and the amount of volunteer or professional help that is available.

Traditional Daytime Wedding Reception
Menu Suggestions

Most caterers figure eight pieces of finger food per person. This may be divided into six tiny tea sandwiches or canapés and two sweets per person. The minimal basic requirements for a wedding reception are twofold—a beverage, which may be a choice of a chilled punch, sparkling grape juice, or hot tea and coffee, and a sweet, which usually consists of a wedding cake.

Other beverage options are:

> Champagne by the glass
> Champagne Punch with fresh strawberries or peaches (in the summer)
> Champagne Fountain
> Hot punches or grogs in the winter
> Wine Punch or Wine by the glass
> Cocktails and Mixed Drinks

REFRESHMENTS: CANAPÉS AND FINGER SANDWICHES

Most people enjoy preparing a wedding reception menu that is a little fancier in appearance than, say, the traditional cocktail party menu. Finger sandwiches may be either open faced or closed. They may be cut into small rounds, triangles, hearts, squares, and oblong shapes using a wide variety of breads—white, whole wheat, rye, or black.

A choice of spreads may be used in the sandwiches or as fillings in miniature puffs, cherry tomatoes, or mushrooms. Some popular mixtures are made of minced turkey or chicken, ham or tongue, chopped olives, salmon, or anchovy spread. Open faced sandwiches may be garnished with a slice of black or green olive, parsley, a strip of red pimento, miniature pickles, or a slice of hard boiled egg.

In addition, you may wish to serve rolled watercress, cucumber, or asparagus sandwiches as well as some canapés such as pinwheels made of bologna or ham and cream cheese.

Hot hors d'ouevres may be passed as well, such as bite size portions of quiche, bacon wrapped around water chestnuts or around a pimento-stuffed olive, carmelized bacon, hot toasted mushroom sandwiches, hot chutney cheese rounds, or cheese puffs made with filo dough and filled with feta cheese, called by its Greek name, *tiropites*. Stuffed eggs seasoned with curry or chutney are always in high demand and so are assorted cheese trays, or lovely vegetable or fresh fruit baskets.

In addition to the wedding cake, a fancy sweet table may be set with three-tiered stands, on which are displayed miniature French pastries, nuts and mints.

Wedding Brunches

These may be served buffet style or guests may be seated at long or round tables. The beverage served may be either wine, champagne, or sparkling grape juice, with a choice of Bloody Marys or Screwdrivers. A tray of stuffed mushrooms, cubes of cheese, or cheese sticks may be offered with the beverage.

Buffet Style

For buffet brunches, luncheons, or suppers, a "forks only" type menu is most convenient, and one buffet table is less costly than several tables that require more food. A variety of molded salads may be displayed on the buffet table, such as tomato or avocado aspic, a chicken or ham salad, a herring or shrimp salad, a curried potato salad, or a marinated vegetable platter. A variety of croissants, rolls, or English muffins may be offered with a choice of jams and jellies. The wedding cake is served for dessert and chocolate mints may be placed on the tables. Hot coffee or tea completes the menu, although in some cases iced tea with mint leaves or iced coffee may be preferred.

A Sit-Down Wedding Brunch

When guests are seated, a glass of fruit juice, a fresh fruit cup, or a half a grapefruit may be waiting at each place setting. The second course may be Eggs Benedict on toast or on English muffins served with Canadian bacon, fresh melon balls or a spiced peach or apple. Miniature pecan rolls or Danish pastries as well as wedding cake may be offered along with a beverage.

A Wedding Luncheon

While guests are going through the receiving line, champagne or Cold Duck may be offered, and hot or cold hors d'ouevres may be passed to the guests or served from a buffet table, everyone helping themselves.

SUGGESTED MENUS

Sit-down Luncheon

MENU #1

1st COURSE: Hot Boullion or Cream Soup
or
Seafood Cocktail or Salad
or
Chilled Melon Balls

2nd COURSE: Chicken or Seafood Crepes
or
Quiche
or
Monte Cristo Sandwiches

DESSERT: Chocolate Truffles
Wedding Cake
Tea and Coffee

Sit-down Luncheon

MENU #2

1st COURSE: Fresh Fruit Cup

2nd COURSE: Boned Breast of Chicken
with
Country Ham (optional)
Mushroom Sauce
Rice Balls

3rd COURSE: Asparagus and Shrimp Salad

DESSERT: Individual Ice Cream Molds
Petit Fours
Wedding Cake
Tea and Coffee

Summer Buffet Supper

Poached Cold Salmon with Dill Sauce
Platters of Cold Sliced Turkey and Roast Beef
Condiments
Fresh Zucchini Vegetable Casserole
Thin Party Breads
Fruits, Melons, and Berries
Macaroons
Wedding Cake
Tea and Coffee

Sit-Down Formal Dinner

1st COURSE: Seafood Cocktail or
Mock Turtle Soup

2nd COURSE: Filet of Beef Tenderloin
with Bearnaise Sauce
Lattice Potatoes
Hot Creamed Spinach with Coconut
Cloverleaf Rolls

3rd COURSE: Hearts of Artichoke Salad

DESSERT: Miniature Fruit Tarts
Wedding Cake
Tea and Coffee

CHAPTER 6

Announcements, Invitations, Stationery

"The horror of that moment" the king went on
"I shall never never forget!"
"You will, though" the queen said,
"if you don't make a memorandum of it."

ALICE IN WONDERLAND BY LEWIS CARROLL

THE GUEST LIST

Making a memorandum of everything connected with a wedding is the best advice I can give you, especially when it comes to guest lists!

Everyone on the guest list, including the parents of the groom, all members of the wedding party, and the clergy-member or judge and his spouse, should be sent invitations through the mail. These will be treasured by all as happy mementos of this particular day. You may wish to mail one to yourselves, too, both for the fun of receiving your own invitation through the mail and checking how long it takes to be delivered.

ADDRESSING INVITATIONS

It's a courtesy to send wedding invitations to both a husband and wife, even when only one member of the couple is known through work or school, or when it's assumed that only one person will be able to attend.

When assembling guest lists from both sides of the family, ask that names be spelled out completely with full addresses, just as they will appear on the envelope, with zip codes. For instance, the list should read, "Mr. and Mrs. John Roger Gallagher" and not, "Mr. and Mrs. J.R. Gallagher." Then, when it is time to address the envelopes, the job will go so much faster.

It may also be helpful both now—and later at the reception—if a duplicate guest list is distributed to both sets of parents. If the parents know all the guests' names and the places where they come from, it will help them to make friendly conversation with people they are meeting for the first time.

Since receptions are by invitation only, if you wish a single person to bring a friend, write, "Please bring a friend" at the bottom of the invitation in matching ink, or "Please bring Mr. Jonathan Belding," if you know the person's name. Better yet, a personal invitation may be sent. An engaged girl may ask to bring her fiancé, and an engaged man may ask to bring his fiancée, and a personal invitation should be sent to each.

Once the wedding list is complete and the hour and date of the wedding are set, it's time to concentrate on the wording and style of the invitations.

INVITATIONS, ANNOUNCEMENTS, INFORMALS

Basically there are three types of stationery to consider, (1) the invitation asking guests to the ceremony and/or reception; (2) the announcement informing friends and relatives that the wedding has taken place; and (3) the informal to be used for thank-you notes, written invitations, or brief messages.

THE INFORMAL HOME WEDDING

For a very small or informal wedding, the bride may telephone or write personal invitations on good stationery, giving the time and place of the wedding:

April 9, 1983

Dear Aunt Mary,
John and I will be married on Saturday, May 1, at two o'clock in my parents' home. We are so anxious to have you be with us and to share our happiness! Please let us know if you can come.

With love,
Susan

Telephone number optional
Return address on the envelope

Or the parents of the bride may write a note:

July 12, 1983

Dear Catherine,
Jennifer and Bob will be married Saturday, August 9 at five o'clock at the Presbyterian Church. We would like you and Jim to come to the ceremony. There will be a small reception afterwards in our condominium, and we look forward to your being with us.

Fondly,
Diane

Telephone number optional
Return address on the envelope

ORIGINAL ARTWORK

Some couples, particularly professional artists, like to design their own wedding invitations. If sufficient time is allowed to complete the job, to address the envelopes, and to mail invitations three or four weeks before the wedding, then the idea of designing original invitations can add that personal touch so important to every wedding.

CALLIGRAPHY

The art of calligraphy is a special skill of writing by hand sometimes used in addressing envelopes and designing invitations. There are many styles to choose from. For wedding invitations or announcements, usually only one copy is hand written, and the original is then taken to a printer to be copied on heavy paper in quantity. For small weddings, each invitation may be written by hand.

ORDERING WEDDING STATIONERY

The invitation reflects the style of the wedding and sets the tone by letting guests know what to expect. An invitation should be factual and concise. It should say who, why, where, and when. Anything else is superfluous. In my opinion, the wedding invitation is not the place to be creative —just state the facts, and let the expressions of love appear in the wedding vows. I feel the same way about hearts and flowers. These belong on the cake!

The best place to order stationery is in a department store, a stationery store, or a jewelry store, preferably one that has an experienced consultant to advise you. Avoid ordering stationery in such places as drug stores because they will print your order exactly as you give it to them—mistakes and all! I know of a couple who carefully checked the names for correct spelling and the date, but on the day of the wedding the phone rang off the hook because no one knew where the wedding was to take place. This bit of information was omitted on the invitation!

There are many weights of paper, shades of color, sizes and styles of script to choose from. Think about the size of

1. Mr. and Mrs. William Smith
   510 Liberty Street
   Oak Park, Illinois 60011

2. Mr. and Mrs. William Smith
   510 Liberty Street
   Oak Park, Illinois, 60011

3. Mr. and Mrs. William Smith
   510 Liberty Street
   Oak Park, Illinois 60011

4. Mr. and Mrs. William Smith
   510 Liberty Street
   Oak Park, Illinois 60011

5. MR. AND MRS. WILLIAM SMITH
   510 LIBERTY STREET
   OAK PARK, ILLINOIS, 60011

6. Mr. and Mrs. William Smith
   510 Liberty Street
   Oak Park, Illinois 60011

SAMPLES OF CALLIGRAPHY STYLES

the invitation, especially if you intend to have something printed in the lower left-hand corner, such as reception information, which requires more space, and for this you need a larger invitation. The same holds true for announcements when you wish to include at-home information in the lower left-hand corner. The quantity of invitations to order depends on the number of guests you are inviting, plus an additional ten or twenty-five in case there are people you may have overlooked. It is much less expensive to order an additional amount with your original order than to reorder! And remember you'll need only *one* invitation per couple—not two.

Raised Lettering and Engraving

Hand engraving on copper plates is very deluxe and most expensive. *Machine engraving*, also done on copper plates, is a process difficult for anyone but an expert to differentiate from hand engraving. The most popular raised-lettering process, and much less expensive, is something referred to as *thermography*. This gives the appearance of engraving, because when you run your finger over the paper, you can feel the lettering. *Printing* is the least expensive and seldom used for weddings.

Coat of Arms

If the family of the bride has a coat of arms and wishes to use it, the crest may be embossed at the top of the first page but not in color. No other marking or device is acceptable. The crest is used only when the parents of the bride or her immediate family issues the invitation or announcement. The husband's full coat of arms is used only when the couple themselves makes the announcement of the marriage.

When to Order and Mail

Invitations need to be mailed three or four weeks before the wedding—four weeks or more should be allowed for mail to guests coming from any distance.

Invitations, therefore, should be ordered six to eight weeks before the wedding, as there is usually a big rush of orders during the popular wedding months of June and September. The envelopes may be ordered in advance, however, so that addressing may be completed before the actual invitations are received. Ordering extra envelopes will come in handy in case some are misaddressed.

Stamps

For that personal touch, check with your post office for commemorative issues that are suitable to use on wedding envelopes for invitations and announcements. Commemorative stamps with birds, flowers, or loving sentiments attract notice, and the recipients will be impressed with this special attention to detail.

The Inner and Outer Envelope

One unique convention for wedding invitations is that two envelopes are used, an outer and an inner envelope. The inner envelope is not sealed. The invitation, folded edge down, and all enclosures are put in the inner envelope bearing only the names of invited guests, such as "Mr. and Mrs. Jackson," with neither the first names nor address. Very intimate relatives may be addressed on the inner envelope in a loving way, such as "Grandmother" or "Aunt Joan and Uncle Paul." Small children's names are written simply, "Curtis and Victoria" or below the parents' name, "Miss

Victoria Jackson," for teenagers. The plural of "Miss" is "Misses," and the plural of "Mr." is "Messrs.", so for more than one young person, names are written, "Misses Victoria and Alicia Jackson" or "Messrs. Curtis and Richard Jackson." Even when a family is living under one roof, it is courteous to send individual invitations to young adults. Older family members *must* receive separate invitations.

The smaller inner envelope is inserted into the larger outer envelope so that the person's name appears when the outer envelope is first opened. Both envelopes are always addressed by hand. Before addressing, avoid any mix up of the inner and outer envelope! This could be a time-consuming and costly mistake.

In addressing the outer envelope, no abbreviations or initials are used, except the words *Mr.* and *Mrs.* The words *street* and *avenue* and the name of the state are not abbreviated.

Mr. and Mrs. John Roger Gallagher
123 Lakeshore Road
Beaver Island, Michigan 49720

Return Addresses

There was a time when it was considered poor taste to put return addresses on wedding invitations, but since the Post Office requests this information (and they even frown on embossing) it's best to have the return address legibly written.

WORDING OF INVITATIONS AND ANNOUNCEMENTS

People who like to follow tradition may be surprised to learn the number of specific rules that are in usage today.

Don't be misled by some unusual examples found in sample stationery albums in stores.

1. The word *honour* is still spelled with a *u*, as in the "honour of your presence" for ceremonies in church or temple.

2. The wording to a ceremony in a home, club, or hotel reads, "the pleasure of your company . . ."

3. No punctuation is used except after abbreviations such as *Mr.* and *Mrs.*, and Jr. The comma is used after the day of the week; for example, "Tuesday, the fifteenth of September." The title *Doctor* is written in full; otherwise abbreviations, initials, or nicknames are never used.

4. The year is optional on wedding invitations but mandatory on announcements. If used, it must be spelled out, but long numbers in a street address may be written in numerals. In a large city, there may be more than one church with the same name. To avoid confusion give the address in the invitation.

5. Half-hours are written as "half after four," never "half past four." The word *o'clock* is always spelled out.

6. An invitation to the wedding ceremony in church does not include an R.S.V.P. (unless followed by a reception), but an invitation to a home wedding always includes an R.S.V.P.

7. On the reception invitation, R.S.V.P. or "The favour of a reply is requested" are both correct. Or if the address to which the reply is to be sent differs from the address on the invitation, you may say, "Kindly send reply to . . ." with the address.

When it comes to the wording of a wedding invitation or announcement, everyone's family relationships are different. If the bride's parents are living, the invitation usually is worded as follows:

> *Mr. and Mrs. Loren Jay Lovejoy*
> *request the honour of your presence*
> *at the marriage of their daughter*
> *Jennifer Anne*
> *to*
> *Mr. Robert William Baldwin*
> *on Saturday, the fifteenth of September*
> *nineteen hundred and eighty-three*
> *at five o'clock*
> *Congregational Church*
> *Berkeley, California*

The year on the wedding invitation is optional, but it is obligatory on the announcement. The year may also be written "one thousand nine hundred and eighty three."

If the bride's mother is a widow, the invitation reads:

> *Mrs. Loren Jay Lovejoy*
> *requests the honour of your presence*
> *at the marriage of her daughter*

If the bride's mother is divorced, it is becoming more usual for the invitation to read:

> *Mrs. Diane Jones Lovejoy*
> *requests the honour of your presence*
> *at the marriage of her daughter*

But the recommended and more traditional way is to combine her maiden name and married surname:

> *Mrs. Jones Lovejoy*

If the bride's mother is divorced and remarried, the invitation reads:

> *Mr. and Mrs. Alexander Glen Wilson*
> *request the honour of your presence*
> *at the marriage of her daughter*
> *Jennifer Anne Lovejoy*

If the bride's stepmother gives the wedding, the invitation reads:

> *Mr. and Mrs. Loren Jay Lovejoy*
> *request the honour of your presence*
> *at the marriage of Mrs. Lovejoy's stepdaughter*
> *Jennifer Anne Walker*

If the bride's mother and father are divorced, and both have remarried, and the parents are friendly and wish to share the wedding expenses and act as cohosts, then both names appear on the invitation. The bride's mother's name appears first:

> *Mr. and Mrs. Alexander Glen Wilson*
> *and*
> *Mr. and Mrs. Loren Jay Lovejoy*
> *request the honour of your presence*
> *at the marriage of*
> *Jennifer Anne Lovejoy*
> *to*

However, it is more usual that the bride's mother issues the invitations to the wedding, while the father might issue the invitations to the reception, if he is paying for it.

If the father is a widower, the invitation reads:

> *Mr. Loren Jay Lovejoy*
> *requests the honour of your presence*
> *at the marriage of his daughter*

If the bride's widowed father has remarried, the invitation reads:

Mr. and Mrs. Loren Jay Lovejoy
request the honour of your presence
at the marriage of his daughter

If a young bride is marrying for the second time and her parents are sending the invitation, her married name is included. However, do not include the word "Mrs." in front of her name.

Mr. and Mrs. Loren Jay Lovejoy
request the honour of your presence
at the marriage of their daughter
Jennifer Lovejoy Baldwin

With second marriages, the bride usually limits attendance at the ceremony to family and special friends. It's especially thoughtful to include any young children of the bride and groom in the wedding party. There's no limit to the number of people who may be invited to the reception.

Wedding invitations may also be issued by a friend or close relative, as well as by an eldest brother or sister, grandparents, or by an aunt and uncle.

Military Titles

When the groom or the bride's father is a member of the army, navy, coast guard, air force, marine corps or on active duty in the reserve force, he uses his military title.

An officer, whose rank is captain in the army or lieutenant, senior grade in the navy or is of higher rank, places his title in front of his name:

Colonel Richard Cromwell
United States Army

Those of lower rank place their name and title as follows:

Richard Cromwell
Ensign, United States Navy

The second line for reserve officers on active duty will read, "Army of the United States" or "United States Naval Reserve." First and second lieutenants in the army both use the word *lieutenant* only.

A noncommissioned officer or enlisted man may have his rank and branch of the service listed below his name or not, as he chooses:

Richard Cromwell
Corporal, Signal Corps, United States Army
or
Richard Cromwell
Apprentice Seaman, United States Naval Reserve

High-ranking officers of the regular armed forces continue to use their titles, followed by their branch of service, even after retirement. A bride who is in the service may use her title if she wishes. When her parents issue the invitation:

Jennifer Anne
Lieutenant, Women's Army Corps

When the couple issues their own invitation:

Jennifer Anne Lovejoy
Lieutenant, Women's Army Corps

Other Titles

Medical doctors, veterinarians, and all persons ordinarily called by their titles will use them on their wedding invitations. Those holding an academic degree do not use their titles, unless the person is in an extremely high position and is always referred to that way. If the person is due to receive a medical degree by the time the wedding takes place, the title should be used on the invitation.

Traditionally, the bride and the bride's mother do not use the title of *Doctor* on the invitation; however this, too, may be changing. If both the bride and groom are doctors the invitation will read:

Dr. Jennifer Anne Lovejoy
and
Dr. Charles Alexander Wilson, etc.

When the Bridegroom's Family Gives the Wedding

There are times when the groom's parents may issue the invitations as follows:

Mr. and Mrs. Loren Jay Lovejoy
request the honour of your presence
at the marriage of
Miss Gloria Niswander
to their son
Henry Loren Lovejoy

Optional wording might be:

Charles Alexander Wilson
son of Mr. and Mrs. Alexander Glen Wilson

The announcement, however, should be sent in the name of the bride's parents, if they are living. Or instead of announcements, the groom's mother may send personal notes with newspaper clippings to her friends.

Invitations by the Bride and Groom's Parents

When the bride and groom's parents cohost the wedding and share in the expenses, it is only fair that both couples' names appear on the invitations:

> *Mr. and Mrs. Loren Jay Lovejoy*
> *and*
> *Mr. and Mrs. Alexander Glen Wilson*
> *request the pleasure of your company*
> *at the marriage of*
> *Jennifer Anne Lovejoy*
> *and*
> *Charles Alexander Wilson, etc.*

In European and other foreign countries, customs different from those I've described are observed, and their delightful practice is sometimes followed here. For example, an invitation may be printed in English on the right-hand side and in another language on the left. Or a double invitation issued by both the bride and groom's parents may be written as follows:

> *Mr. and Mrs. Ricardo Gonzalez*
> *request the honour of your presence*
> *at the marriage of their daughter*
> *Carlotta*
> *to*
> *Mr. Francesco Romanez, etc.*

> *Mr. and Mrs. Roberto Romanez*
> *request the honour of your presence*
> *at the marriage of their son*
> *Francesco*
> *to*
> *Miss Carlotta Gonzalez, etc.*

Double Weddings

When two sisters have a double ceremony, the older sister is mentioned first, and the invitation reads:

> *Mr. and Mrs. Loren Jay Lovejoy*
> *request the honour of your presence*
> *at the marriage of their daughters*
> *Jennifer Anne*
> *to*
> *Mr. Robert William Baldwin*
> *and*
> *Glenna Julia*
> *to*
> *Mr. Gregory Charles Fitzpatrick*

If the brides are not sisters, the parents names are listed in alphabetical order.

Your Own Invitations

There are numerous occasions when couples prefer to issue their own invitations; for example, when both the bride and groom are living away from home in another city and have set up lives of their own. This is one of the exceptions when the word *Miss* is used before the bride's name, and the invitation reads as follows:

> *The honour of your presence*
> *is requested*
> *at the marriage of*
> *Miss Jennifer Ann Lovejoy*
> *to*   [or *and*]
> *Mr. Jackson Ray Dilworth*

For second marriages the invitation reads:

The pleasure of your company
is requested
at the marriage of
Jennifer Lovejoy Baldwin
to   [or *and*]
Jackson Ray Dilworth

Insert Cards

There is a variety of cards that may be inserted into the fold of an invitation—reception invitations, pew cards, response cards, and at-home cards. When one uses insert cards, it's best to use folded invitations, because it has been learned from experience that when invitations are not folded, the insert cards sometimes remain left unnoticed inside the envelope. Unfortunately, this results in hurt feelings, especially when people think they have not been invited to the reception.

RECEPTION INVITATIONS

When the reception takes place immediately after the ceremony in church, there is room on the invitation to say: "Reception Immediately Following Ceremony."

But when the reception is held in a different location from the ceremony, a separate card is inserted in the invitation. And if it is to be a breakfast, brunch, luncheon, cocktail supper, buffet, or dinner, it is especially considerate to say so explicitly. Grateful guests will be able to plan their schedules accordingly! A sample reception card may read as follows:

Judge and Mrs. Edwin Eisendrath II
request the pleasure of your company
at the wedding breakfast
following the ceremony
Pierre Hotel
New York City

R.S.V.P.   [note the word *breakfast*]

The letters R.S.V.P. or Rsvp come from the abbreviated French phrase, *Répondez, s'il vous plaît*, meaning please respond. Or the card may read:

Dinner Reception
immediately following the ceremony
Berkshire Country Club
Rolling Hills, Kentucky

The favour of a reply is requested
Old Orchard Lane
Blue Lake, Kentucky

[note the word *dinner*]

It is not necessary to write either "R.S.V.P." or "the favour of a reply is requested," if one uses a response card. The card itself is obviously a request for an answer.

One may say "adults only" on the lower left-hand corner of the reception card. This usually means young people sixteen years or older are included. In case of doubt guests may check with the hostess.

THE RESPONSE CARD

This little card has crept into our lifestyle for the convenience of guests—it prompts them to reply at once. And for the convenience of the host, it is imperative for him to know the exact head count for two reasons: (1) No one likes to sit next to an empty chair, and (2) the host is billed whether the guest is there or not.

The matching response card and envelope with the return address printed on it may be stamped or not. It may read as follows:

The favour of a reply is requested
by June 1, 1983 [date optional]

M   _____

    will   _____   *attend*

Or it may read:

Please respond on or before June 1, 1983 [date optional]

M   _____

    will   _____   *attend*

THE PEW CARDS

For very large weddings, this little 2-by-3-inch card invites special guests or close relatives to be seated in a reserved row in the pew section marked with ribbons or flowers. (Seats are not numbered within these rows.) On the card is printed "within the ribbon" or "groom's reserved section." Instead of a printed pew card, the bride's mother may sign her name on a calling card, with all the necessary information written on the back. The pew card is mailed after guests have accepted the invitation to the wedding. An engraved pew card may also read:

_____ [handwritten]
will present this card to the usher
Blessed Sacrament Cathedral
Pew Number

_____ [handwritten]

AT-HOME CARDS

These are usually ordered at the same time as the invitations and announcements and may be included with the announcements or mailed after the wedding. At-home cards give the new street address, city, state, and zip code. It is not necessary to send at-home cards unless the couple is permently settled. When the at-home card is included in the invitation it reads as follows:

After the first of August
Old Orchard Lane
Houston, Texas 77000

When it is included with the announcement it reads:

Mr. and Mrs. Robert William Baldwin
after the first of August
Old Orchard Lane
Houston, Texas 77000

Instead of sending a separate card, the at-home information may be placed on the lower left-hand corner of the announcement.

WEDDING ANNOUNCEMENTS

These are mailed only to people who have not been invited to the wedding, yet who would like to be informed of the marriage. In the case of a home wedding, for example, the number of guests may of necessity be limited to a small group. Announcements may be mailed to people who live far away, or acquaintances one hasn't seen in a long time. A wedding announcement does not require a gift, so there's no need to hesitate in sending announcements. Wedding announcements may be sent by the parents of the bride or by both parents of the bride and groom, or by any close relative, or by the couple themselves, the same as invitations:

Miss Jennifer Anne Lovejoy
and
Mr. Robert William Baldwin
announce their marriage
on Sunday, the fourteenth of February
nineteen hundred and eighty three
Palm Beach, Florida

A DEATH IN THE IMMEDIATE FAMILY

When a very old person, such as a grandparent, has requested that arrangements for the wedding not be changed in the event of their death, then the wedding may take place as originally scheduled.

If there is a sudden death in the immediate family, a notice may be sent immediately to the newspaper in case of postponement, and the invitations may be recalled by telephone or telegram. If time permits, a printed card may be sent:

Mr. and Mrs. James Longworth Phillips
regret that due to a death in the family
the invitation to
their daughter's wedding
[names are optional]
on Saturday, the fourth of June
must be recalled

Wedding invitations to a large wedding may be recalled, but the wedding may still take place with only a few close friends and relatives present. Much depends on the feelings of the immediate family.

MULTIPURPOSE INFORMALS

These small foldover notes are used for a great many purposes, including thank-you notes for shower gifts, wedding gifts, and invitations. The bride's name may be engraved or imprinted, or she may use her initials before the wedding. Her new name or initials are used for notes written after the wedding. A popular new custom is to use the initial of the surname of the couple, which is large and centered, with the smaller initials of the bride's and groom's given names on either side.

PRINTED MENUS

For formal luncheons or dinners, a menu of the meal may be placed at each table. This may be hand-lettered or printed and artistically decorated with a floral pattern if desired. Individual souvenir menus may also be placed on the plate in front of each guest. I have before me a souvenir menu printed in green on a four inch by eleven inch yellow ribbon of silk. On this is printed the name of the hotel with its crest, the bride's and groom's names, the menu, the wines, and—at the very bottom—the name of the city and the date.

PRINTED ACKNOWLEDGMENT CARDS

For very large weddings, it is helpful to have cards printed that acknowledge the receipt of a gift. The bride, then, is not under such heavy pressure to write her personal thank-you notes. The card may say:

Mrs. _____
has received your wedding gift and
will take pleasure in writing you
later of her appreciation.

Here are some helpful tips to remember when writing a thank-you note:

1. Write the date on the note. Sometimes mail is delayed through no fault of yours.
2. Mention the name of the gift. The person who gave you the candleholder would like to know that you remember this particular gift and who it came from.
3. Mention something nice about the gift. If the only thing you like about the gift is the design or color, then mention the design or color.
4. Mention your fiancé's name (or fiancée, as the case may be).
5. Sign only one name to the note, since only one person actually writes it. Be warm and friendly in closing by saying *Love* or *Affectionately* or *Cordially*, depending on how well you know the person. *Sincerely* sounds too cold.
6. Mail thank-you notes as soon as possible, or the giver will become anxious and concerned that your present has gone astray.

May 15, 1983

Dear Connie,

Richard and I are thrilled with the brass candleholder! The Early American design will be absolutely perfect in our new home. Thank you so much for this lovely gift.

Affectionately,
Jennifer

Oct. 1, 1983

Dear Jim,

Betty and I are enjoying the coffee grinder you gave us so much! We both thank you for your useful gift and hope you will be able to share a good cup of coffee with us soon. Our best wishes to you and Jane.

Cordially,
Bill

DETERMINING A WOMAN'S NAME
AFTER MARRIAGE

This is a good time to devote some thought to the way a woman is going to sign her name after marriage.

In the past, it has been the social custom that when Jennifer Anne Lovejoy marries Robert William Baldwin for her to sign herself as either Mrs. Robert Baldwin or Jennifer Lovejoy Baldwin. And many couples agree this is the best choice today.

Nevertheless, a woman does have other options open to her. The fact is not generally known that a married woman is entitled, but not legally compelled, to use her husband's surname. There is no state except Hawaii that has a law stating that a woman must take her husband's name upon marriage. For professional women, keeping the name by which they have become identified is an important option. A woman with an established career is reluctant to trade her names for that of her husband. She may suffer a loss of identity and create confusion among customers, clients, or constituents. On the other side, women whose husbands are well-respected socially or professionally are often eager to adopt their husbands' surnames and attach them to their own names as embellishment, gaining the best of both worlds. Other women simply have a deep desire to keep their own names, which legally may be retained on their driver's licenses, car registrations, deeds to property, voting records, and even may be passed on to their children.

Some couples adopt hyphenated names. For example, Jennifer and Robert will become Jennifer Lovejoy-Baldwin and Robert Lovejoy-Baldwin. It must be mentioned that when dealing with government agencies, some computers may not be programmed to accept hyphenated names, in which case it is necessary to insist that agencies hand type the records.

If a couple decides that the wife will retain her own name, a card may be enclosed with the invitations or announcements, which may also include the at-home information:

Jennifer Anne Lovejoy
wishes to announce that she
will retain her birth-given name
for all legal and social purposes
after her marriage to
Robert William Baldwin
The understanding and cooperation
of friends and relatives would
be greatly appreciated

After the first of July
323 Bridge Street
Portland, Maine 04110

OUT-OF-TOWN RECEPTIONS

When one set of parents lives in another community and wishes to have their friends meet the bride or groom either before or after the wedding, a reception may be planned and the wording may be formal or informal.

Formal wording (before the wedding):

> *Mr. and Mrs. Loren Jay Lovejoy*
> *request the pleasure of your company*
> *at a buffet supper in honor of*
> *Miss Jennifer Anne Lovejoy*
> *and*
> *Mr. Robert William Baldwin*
> *on Saturday, the fifteenth of October*
> *at seven o'clock*
> *Rolling Hills Country Club*
> *Kansas City*

The favour of a reply is requested   Black Tie

Informal wording on a foldover invitation (after the wedding):

Mr. and Mrs. Loren Jay Lovejoy   (outside)

> *You are cordially invited*   (inside)
> *to a cocktail reception*
> *in honour of*
> *Jennifer and Robert Baldwin*
> *on Wednesday, the fifth of June*
> *from five until seven o'clock*
> *100 Greenway Drive*

Regrets only

CHAPTER 7

Attendants in the Wedding Party

Laughter is the sunshine of the soul
RALPH WALDO EMERSON

CHOOSING THE ATTENDANTS

Choosing the attendants for a wedding can at times be very simple, pleasant, and uncomplicated. It's so easy for the bride to invite a best friend or sister to be maid or matron of honor or for the groom to invite a brother or best friend to be his best man.

There are times, however, when complications arise that require creative solutions. Let's suppose the bride has twin sisters. Or the groom is one of triplets. Or the best friend announces she is pregnant and her due date coincides with the wedding date. Or one of the attendants is transferred out of the country. In the case of a second marriage, a father may want both of his sons to share equally in the ceremony as best man.

What to do?

It is perfectly possible to have two maids of honor or matrons of honor or two best men as attendants. They share all responsibilities, the older having first choice. When the bride or groom has a young brother or sister between the ages of five and eight they may be included as flower girl or ring bearer at a formal wedding. Young nieces and nephews or children from a previous marriage will feel very welcome and special to be included as part of the wedding party. Boys and girls over eight may be invited to be junior bridesmaids or groomsmen.

When someone drops out of the wedding party due to unforeseen circumstances, it's perfectly acceptable to ask a friend to step in, even at the last minute. A true friend, if she's able to oblige, will gladly say yes!

THE INFORMAL WEDDING

For a small ceremony at home, in church, or in a judge's chambers, the bride may ask only a maid or matron of honor to be her attendant. Usually this is either a sister or one of her close friends. The groom may invite a best man to be by his side. This may be a brother or a best friend.

THE DUTIES OF THE MAID OR
MATRON OF HONOR

The most important duty is to be supportive to the bride before and on the wedding day. She may be invited to shop with the bride or assist in addressing invitations and announcements. She is invited to all the parties and may give one herself.

On the wedding day she arrives early at the bride's house and helps the bride dress, gives her encouragement, and soothes frayed nerves. She will keep track of the hour and do what she can to get everyone to the ceremony on time. When a wedding takes place at home or in the garden, she remembers to take the telephone off the hook during the ceremony! If there is a double-ring ceremony, she holds the groom's ring and hands it to the bride. She also signs her name to the marriage license as a witness. During a more formal wedding, she holds the bride's bouquet, helps adjust her veil and rearranges the train when the bride turns to leave at the end of the service. She stands next to the couple in the receiving line. She is seated on the groom's left at the bridal table and helps the bride change into her going-away outfit.

THE DUTIES OF THE BEST MAN

Next to the bride and groom, the best man is the most important member of the wedding party. He may offer to help the groom pack for his honeymoon and even deliver the luggage of both the newlyweds to the airport and see that it is properly checked on the day of the wedding. He must remember to give the baggage claim checks to the groom and be sure the groom has his traveler's checks, boat or plane tickets, car keys, etc. If the couple is staying at a nearby hotel or motel, he may register for the couple and give the room key to the groom.

Before the ceremony he is responsible for the groom's being dressed and on time. He is in charge of keeping the wedding ring until the minister asks for it. He keeps the wedding license and the minister's fee available in his own pocket. He sees to it that the check is made out to the minister and not the church. He gives the check in an envelope to the minister before the ceremony or immediately after the recessional. He may also give out envelopes in payment to the organist, soloist, sexton, and altar boys. He signs the marriage license as a witness. The couple is not legally married unless the marriage license is signed by the minister, the bride and groom, and two witnesses.

Just before the church ceremony, he enters from the vestry immediately after the groom and stands behind the groom and slightly to the left, so that he can conveniently give the wedding ring to him when the minister calls for it.

At the end of the service, he may either walk out with the maid or matron of honor or leave through a side door while the procession goes up the aisle. He goes quickly to the front of the church, gives the groom his hat and coat, if needed, and helps the bride and groom into their car. Unless there is a driver, he may drive them to the reception, or he may stay behind and check that there are no stray guests in need of a taxi or transportation to the reception.

At the reception, the best man mingles with the guests. If there is a sit-down meal, he is seated to the bride's right. He proposes the first toast to the bride and groom. This toast may be extremely brief: "To Jennifer and Bill—may they share a long and happy life together!" or it may be humorous and sentimental, but it should always be in good taste. If the best man acts as master-of-ceremonies, he introduces the speakers and announces the start of the cake-cutting ceremony.

The best man dances with the bride after the groom, her father-in-law, and her father have had their turns.

At the end of the reception, he helps the groom out of his wedding clothes. When the couple is ready to leave the reception, he escorts the groom's family to the dressing room to say goodbye. He then leads the couple through the waiting guests to the exit and escorts them to their car. He checks again that the luggage is in the car and may even drive them to the motel or airport. Or he may return to the reception and relax after a job well done.

THE SEMIFORMAL WEDDING

In addition to the maid or matron of honor and the best man, any number of bridesmaids and ushers may be invited to be part of the wedding party. The attendants are usually close in age, and it is perfectly correct to have married bridesmaids, even if their husbands are not included in the wedding party. However, husbands are asked to all the wedding and rehearsal parties, of course.

The bridesmaids are all close friends or relatives of the bride, and the groom's sister may be included. It is also possible to have two maids or matrons of honor who share responsibilities. One may be in charge of the ring, and the other may help the bride with her veil and train. Bridesmaids have few duties to perform at the wedding except to add charm and beauty to the ceremony and mingle cheerfully with the guests at the reception and to be generally helpful.

The ushers are usually close friends or relatives, and the brother of the bride is often included. They may be married or single, and if married, their wives are invited to attend all the wedding parties. The usher's responsibility is to attend the rehearsal and to arrive properly attired at the church forty-five minutes to one hour ahead of time. Ushers seat the guests who arrive about twenty minutes before the ceremony. For a small wedding there are usually two ushers, and, as a general rule of thumb, there is one usher for every fifty guests. One usher may be asked to act as head usher.

The boutonnieres for the ushers and the bouquets for the bridesmaids are waiting for them at the church.

The ushers line up on the left side of the entrance so they may offer their right arm to the women guests.

As the guests enter, one usher at a time steps forward and asks if they are friends of the bride or groom. He accompanies the bride's relatives and friends to their seats on the left side of the aisle and the groom's relatives and friends to the right side of the aisle. (In Orthodox synagogues the seating is reversed.) At weddings where the great majority of guests are friends of one family, it is perfectly proper to seat guests on either side of the aisle to make the congregation look more balanced.

The usher offers his right arm to each woman and escorts her down the aisle to her seat. If a man is accompanying a woman, he follows a step or two behind. If two women arrive together, he escorts the elder woman down the aisle to her seat. Men alone simply walk with the usher to their seats. When many guests are waiting, one or two guests may walk down the aisle behind the usher.

It's nice when the ushers exchange a few friendly remarks as they escort wedding guests to their seats. Any pleasant comment about the weather, mutual friends, or whatever is welcome. After guests are seated, one or two ushers will roll out the white carpet, if one is being used, and lay it down the aisle. Then the head usher escorts the bride's mother to the front left-hand pew, and this is the signal to the congregation that the ceremony is about to begin.

Tardy guests are not ushered to seats, but occupy pews at the back. The ushers then lead the processional, as arranged at the rehearsal. After the ceremony they take their designated place in the recessional. They then return to the front pews and escort the unescorted women of the immediate families to the front door.

THE FORMAL WEDDING

There are usually more attendants at a formal wedding, and these may include junior bridesmaids, a flower girl, and a ring bearer. The ushers may also have more responsibilities, such as removing the pew bows that are used to identify the reserved seats. After guests are seated, the ribbons are replaced.

For a candlelight ceremony, two ushers light the candles about fifteen minutes before the ceremony starting at the back of the church. They slowly move down the aisle together, lighting each candle on the left and right side of the aisle with tapers.

RESERVED PEWS

It is most important to reserve several front pews on each side of the center aisle for the immediate family and close friends. The people who sit here are either notified by word of mouth or by a pew card to be presented to the usher. Or ushers may be given a list of special pew holders in case guests have forgotten their pew cards.

USHERS AT THE RECEPTION

Ushers can make themselves very useful by helping to introduce guests to one another, dancing with single women, keeping an eye on youngsters, or helping the photographer assemble his subjects for group photographs. In addition, their help may be needed in getting guests off to the airport or escorting the bridesmaids to their homes when the party is over.

CHAPTER 8

What to Wear

Something old something new
Something borrowed something blue

DRESS FOR THE WEDDING PARTY

The formality of the bride's gown dovetails with the outfits worn by the men in the wedding party. Therefore, before the bride has the pleasure of selecting her own gown, she needs to decide the type of wedding that is planned—informal, semiformal, or formal; the time of day; and the season of the year. The formality and the season both dictate the length of the skirt, the style of the dress, the colors, and fabrics. The time of day dictates what the men in the wedding party wear.

It's best if the bride and groom discuss their dress preferences together ahead of time. Then when the bride goes shopping for her gown, she is in a much better position to plan the total effect of the entire wedding party, so that everyone will be in harmony for a lovely, long-lasting group photograph.

THE WEDDING GOWN

Here again the bride has innumerable choices. She can buy a dress off the rack and have it altered to fit, or, given enough time, she can custom-order a gown from a bridal salon. She may decide to wear her mother's wedding gown or a treasured family heirloom. She may borrow a gown or even rent one, which is just as practical nowadays as for a groom to rent his suit. She may prefer to wear an ethnic original from her homeland—an Indian sari, a Mexican wedding dress, or a Japanese kimono. Or she can lovingly sew her own or have a talented dressmaker design one for her.

There are several books available that give explicit directions with diagrams on how to sew your own wedding dress. One paperback written by Gail Brown and Karen Dillon, published by Palmer/Pletsch Associates, Portland, Oregon, is in its second printing.

Some of the large fabric stores not only have a wide selection of beautiful fabrics, along with both imported and domestic laces, but they also have the names of reliable dressmakers they are willing to recommend.

One experienced seamstress explained to me that she combines two or three patterns, and if the bride is away at school, for instance, she makes up a muslin sample and mails it to the bride for fitting. The result is a fashionable original at a fraction of the cost of a dress purchased in a fine store.

And as for color, the bride may choose any color that suits her fancy—white, ivory, or pastel. (Chinese brides wear red!) Every spring and fall, bridal salons receive new styles that reflect current fashions. Shopping for clothes for the bride and her attendants may begin three to six months before the wedding for special orders. This allows time for fittings and newspaper photographs.

Large department stores put on extravagant bridal fashion shows with up-to-the-minute styles currently available on the market. Attending these is one way to size up the total picture of what is offered for the entire wedding party in colors, fabrics, styles, and designs. Often it firms up in the bride's own mind not only what she likes, but what she doesn't like!

After looking around at several bridal salons, it's best for the bride to make an appointment with the salon of her choice. She should talk frankly and openly with the salesperson about her requirements and the limit she intends to spend. As they work on commission, most salespersons begin by showing their most expensive lines first. It's terribly hard for the bride to resist a dream of a dress that is tempting beyond her means. Better to select two or three favorites and then return to see the dresses again before making a final selection.

If she is buying a gown to match an heirloom veil, she should bring the veil to the salon so that any off-white shade can be matched to an ivory or pastel shade gown.

The Pregnant Bride

Bridal salons do not advertise the fact that they carry special lines of wedding gowns that are complimentary to the pregnant bride, but they do! Most brides advise the fitter of their pregnancy during the first appointment, which saves extra alterations on the final fitting and is much appreciated by the fitter.

The Second Time Around

Today's bride is older, more career oriented, and more sophisticated than in the past. She knows exactly what she wants. Thirty percent of all weddings are second marriages, and the fashion industry is taking notice of this fact. The bridal wear industry is introducing lines of "informal gowns" that are usually off-white or pastel-colored and mid-calf to ankle-length with no train.

What the bride wears the second time around depends greatly on her age and the circumstances of her first wedding. Let's take a very young woman who eloped and whose marriage was annulled. In her case, there's no reason she could not enjoy a truly formal wedding with all the trimmings. On the other hand, there's the woman who had an enormous church wedding with hundreds of guests a few years ago. Should she remarry, it is in far better taste for her to have a few close friends to a private ceremony followed by a reception, if she chooses. Then there is the bride who was happily married for many years. She has grown children and possibly grandchildren. Everyone is delighted at the prospect of her remarriage. A lovely semiformal wedding is certainly in order here. The bride would choose a dressy off-white or pastel colored gown of mid-calf length without a train. She could wear a hat or flowers in her hair. All the couple's friends are invited to the ceremony as well as to the reception.

Preserving the Gown

After the wedding, the bride arranges for someone to take the gown to a reliable dry cleaner. There are cleaners who will pack the gown in an airtight box. This process, which is costly, preserves the gown so that it may be worn again on a special anniversary or kept for future wear by other members of the family.

The Train

The formality of the wedding is not determined by the length of the train. There are various types of trains, including the cathedral train, which is about three to six yards long; the chapel train, which is very full and about eight to twelve inches long; and the sweep train, which is part of the dress and barely sweeps the floor.

The Veil

A variety of material is available for a veil, which can flow to the shoulder, waist, or floor. Shorter veils are lovely, when the detail of the back of the dress is particularly interesting. Sometimes a long veil doubles as a train permitting the design of the dress to show through.

Veils may be held in place with a circlet of pearls or flowers, by hairpins concealed by a tiny bunch of fresh flowers, or by a diamond tiara.

Hair Styles

Some brides like to do their own hair and wear it naturally. Other brides like to do something special on this memorable day. If the bride plans to have her hair styled at a posh beauty salon, she should make an appointment well in advance. She may let the operator do her hair once before the wedding to get the feel of its thickness and texture. If the bride is wearing a veil, she should bring it to the salon so the hair can be suitably styled. The operator will also want to know the lines of the dress—low or high neckline, the length of sleeves—in order to create an elegant head-to-toe look.

Many brides prefer having fresh flowers and/or ribbons twined in a braid instead of wearing veils. Some long-lasting fresh flowers are rosebuds, miniature carnations, gardenias, statice, and daisies. Baby's breath is very effective, because it vibrates alluringly when the bride moves. One can also combine real baby's breath with silk flowers. If the bridesmaids are agreeable, everyone might wear their hair in the same graceful style, either shoulder length or up in a chignon or twist. It may be more convenient in this case to have a hairdresser come to the home and arrange everyone's hair before the wedding.

ATTENDANTS' GOWNS

It is the bride's privilege to choose the design, the material, and the color of the attendants' dresses to complement her own. The gowns may be purchased in a bridal salon, or the bride may suggest the name of a dressmaker who will make all the dresses for the wedding party. Or the bride may provide the patterns for the bridesmaids. For a small, informal wedding, with one or two attendants, she may approve of an outfit that the girls already own. But for a larger wedding, the selecting of gowns for the bridesmaids, the maid or matron of honor, and any junior bridesmaids or flower girls, needs special consideration. The bride ought to consider how the gown will look on the bridesmaid, not only for style and color but also for her age. A dress that is charming on an eighteen-year-old might make a bridesmaid over thirty feel silly. And since the bridesmaids pay for their own dresses, it is considerate to select a style that is within the bridesmaid's budget and may be used after the wedding. If there is a money problem, the bride may offer to pay for a portion of the dress as a gift to the bridesmaid; however, if she does this for one, she should do it for all.

The dress chosen for the maid or matron of honor is usually a different color, although of the same style. Her gown may be a deeper tone, or her dress and bouquet may be the reverse of the bridesmaids.

A junior bridesmaid may wear a gown similar in design to the other bridesmaids, or she may wear a dress that is complementary in style and color to the rest of the bridal party.

The flower girl's dress should be suitable to her age and harmonize with the bridesmaids' gowns in color and fabric.

The ring bearer may wear any color suit, dark in the

winter and light in the summer. Short pants are preferred, because long trousers make a child look too much like a midget.

The most important point to remember in selecting clothing for young people is that they often grow unexpectedly and rapidly. It's best not to have any final fittings until just prior to the wedding. One final point, the parents of the young attendants pay for the purchase or rental of the wedding outfits.

BRIDESMAIDS' SHOES

If the shoes are to be dyed, they should all be done in one store in order to have an exact match. If the bridesmaids live in different cities, they may either buy their shoes and mail them to the bride to have dyed, or they may shop at the same chain store and select both their shoes and dye color by number. A lot of time, trouble, and money is saved by simply wearing white, silver, or gold slippers instead of dying shoes to match the gown.

THE MOTHER OF THE BRIDE

As hostess, the bride's mother stands first in the receiving line, and her dress as well as that of the groom's mother should blend with the rest of the wedding party. She usually selects her dress first and notifies the groom's mother of the color and style. The bride's mother's dress may be as fashionable and becoming as any dress in her wardrobe, one she can wear happily on future occasions. The only restrictions are against black or white. Black is the color for mourning and white is reserved for the bride.

THE GROOM'S FATHER

The groom's father may wear the same costume as the groom and attendants, especially if he plans to stand in the receiving line. Otherwise, he may wear the same suits as the men guests.

MEN'S FORMAL RENTAL CLOTHING

For more reasons than one, the wedding rental business has filled a long-standing gap. With our casual lifestyle, few men own tuxedos or formal dress suits. Secondly, the wedding party looks much more attractive and uniform when all the men are dressed alike. And, finally, it gives the bride and groom a much greater selection of styles and colors, both in the summer and winter.

There are numerous places where one can rent a wide selection of men's clothing—coats, trousers, shirts, vests, ties or ascots and cummerbund. Everything except underwear and socks! There are fashionable men's clothing stores and bridal salons that rent men's outfits. Or one can look in the bridal magazines for locations of shops in major cities.

All rental shops do not carry the same brand nor the same quality of formal wear, nor are all suits in the same excellent condition. Therefore prices vary. Again, it's wise to check around before committing oneself.

Before Six O'Clock

Traditionally, tuxedos are not worn in the daytime, and it's not recommended, but I must admit that all over the country the tuxedo at noon is a common sight today at many weddings.

After Six O'Clock

By the same token, dress code rules for formal weddings are also frequently bent. The white tie and tails are rarely worn even for formal weddings.

How to Rent Men's Formal Suits

There are two routes to go when it comes to renting men's formal dress suits. (1) For the traditional stroller or cutaway with striped trousers (worn in the daytime), or black tuxedo or tails (worn in the evening), the men in the wedding party can all visit the same men's store, if they all live in the same city. But if they live in various sections of the country, they can all rent their traditional conservative suits in their own city and have them properly fitted in advance. (2) The other route is to have everyone measured in a men's shop of their choice and mail the correct measurements to the bride or groom, who will reserve the suits for the final fitting.

Once the couple have made their selections, the rental shop gives the bride and groom forms to pass on to the out-of-town members of the wedding party, and it is their responsibility to gather up the forms and return them to the rental store all at the same time for processing. The form includes the name of the couple, the style of the formal wear, the date of the wedding, the ushers' names, and the measurements.

Measurements are required for the chest, waist, height, trouser inseam, shirt size, and sleeve inseam. Only an experienced person knows how to take these measurements correctly. For example, when measuring an athlete with large thighs and calves and a slim waist, it's far better to order a larger size trouser and take a tuck in the waist, than to order trousers according to waist measure that bind in the leg.

SEMI-FORMAL DAY WEDDING	FORMAL DAY WEDDING	SEMI-FORMAL EVENING WEDDING	FORMAL EVENING WEDDING	SUMMER EVENING WEDDING
Stroller	Cutaway	Tuxedo	Fulldress	Summer Formal

Oxford gray stroller coat, worn with striped trousers, gray double-breasted waistcoat, four-in-hand tie with turn-down collar shirt, plain toe black shoes, gray suede or mocha gloves, black or gray Homburg, pearl stickpin, gold, pearl or stone studs and links.

Oxford gray cutaway, worn with gray double-breasted waistcoat, striped trousers, silk ascot with wing collar or four-in-hand with turn-down collar, plain toe black shoes, gray suede gloves, silk top hat, pearl stickpin, gold, pearl or stone cuff links and studs.

Tuxedo worn with white pleated or pique front shirt with turn-down collar, plain black or midnight blue bow tie with matching cummerbund, black shoes, Homburg, gray suede gloves if desired.

Full Dress worn with matching white pique shirt, waistcoat, bow tie and wing collar. Plain toe black shoes, white gloves, white studs and cuff links.

White dinner jacket, worn with black or midnight blue trousers, black or midnight blue cummerbund and matching bow tie, black pumps or oxfords, white pleated or pique front shirt with turn-down collar, light-weight straw hat, gold or pearl studs and links.

Suspenders

Although there are several built-in adjustments in rental suits, some suppliers provide grey or black and white suspenders. This is an advantage because suspenders prevent pants from slipping below the vest—a separation that shows off an expanse of shirt and does not give a trim appearance.

Ascots

Only when the groomsmen own their own suits does the groom select the ascots and send identical ones to each member of the wedding party as a gift.

Gloves

At informal weddings, none of the men wear gloves. At a formal wedding, ushers always wear gloves, although the groom and best man may not. If the groom does wear gloves, he hands them to the best man while they are standing in the chapel before the ceremony, and the best man tucks both pairs of gloves into his pocket.

Studs and Cufflinks

Ruffled shirts don't need studs, but cufflinks and studs are available for rent with dress shirts.

Shoes

Some men own nothing but a pair of loafers and tennis shoes. Fortunately, shoes are available to rent in most stores for those who want them.

Colors

When selecting a pastel shade in a contemporary suit, especially blue, it cannot be assumed that this tone will automatically be a good match with the bridesmaids' gowns. Be sure to check the color of the gown with the color of the suit and even ask for swatches, which are available from the rental store.

DRESS FOR THE INFORMAL WEDDING

This may take place at home, in city hall, in the clergy-member's study, a friend's home, a club, or any congenial setting. The ceremony may be restricted to close relatives and friends, or in the case of a second marriage may include the children of either or both parties. The ceremony may be followed by a reception to which additional friends are invited.

The bride and her attendants may wear dressy suits or short cocktail dresses in the daytime. The groom wears a dark suit and tie in the winter and a light suit and tie or a navy jacket with white trousers in the summer. In hot climates, he may choose a white suit.

After Six O'Clock

In the evening the bride may choose to wear a long dress, in which case the groom, his attendants, and the bride's father may wear either a dark suit in the winter, a light suit in the summer, or a tuxedo.

DRESS FOR THE SEMIFORMAL WEDDING

This may take place at home, in church, in a private club, hotel, or public facility. For both daytime and evening, the bride wears a long wedding gown, veil optional. Her attendants wear any fashionable length bridesmaid gowns.

Before Six O'Clock

The groom, his attendants, and the bride's father wear a sack coat or stroller with black and grey striped trousers, grey waistcoat, white shirt with turned down collar with four-in-hand tie, and black smooth-toe shoes with black socks. Grey gloves and black or grey homburg hat are optional. White, black, brown, navy, maroon, or pastel tuxedos are also worn for daytime weddings. There is no hard and fast rule as to tuxedo color choices, but in general darker colors are considered best for winter or evening and lighter colors appropriate for summer or morning.

For Evening Weddings

After six o'clock, in the winter, the groom, his attendants, and the bride's father wear either a black, navy blue, brown, or maroon tuxedo. In the summer, white, cream, or pastel jacket with a pleated or piqué soft shirt; cummerbund; black or midnight-blue bow tie; and black patent leather or kid shoes are worn. Grey suede gloves are optional.

THE MOST FORMAL WEDDING

Before or after six o'clock, the bride and her attendants all wear long gowns. The bride's dress has a train, and her veil may be any length.

The mothers of the bride and groom may wear short or long dresses in the daytime and usually long dresses or short cocktail dresses in the evening.

Before Six O'Clock

The groom, his attendants and the bride's father wear cutaway coats, striped trousers, a waistcoat, shirt with winged collar, and a silk ascot or grey and black striped four-in-hand. Black silk socks and black kid shoes. Top hat and grey gloves optional.

After Six O'Clock

The groom and attendants wear full dress black tail coat and trousers, a white bow tie, white gloves, black silk socks, black patent-leather shoes or pumps. A top hat is optional. Or the groomsmen may wear matching tuxedos. In the summer, all the men in the wedding party may wear dinner jackets instead of tails in the evening.

THE MILITARY WEDDING

The military wedding is like any other wedding, except the groom and his attendants are in uniform, and they do not wear boutonnieres. The style of uniform depends on the hour of the ceremony, the type of wedding, and the season of the year. Dress blues or whites are worn during the day and in formal weddings. In the evening, the mess uniform is worn, and for very formal evening weddings the evening dress uniform is worn.

CHAPTER 9

Flowers

My love is like a red red rose
That's newly sprung in June;
Oh, my love is like the melodie
That's sweetly played in tune.

ROBERT BURNS

Flowers add beauty, fragrance, and distinction to every wedding. Moreover, this is a budget item that, with a little imagination, can be controlled in several ways: select flowers in season from a florist whose work you like; look around for nonprofessional help; combine professional and nonprofessional help; or consider sharing expenses with another couple having a wedding on the same day in the same place.

THE PROFESSIONAL FLORIST

Arranging flowers for weddings is a time-consuming and exacting job; therefore it's important to select a florist that specializes in weddings. The ideal person, whether male or female, is artistic, patient, reliable, and experienced. Time is needed for consultation; special orders require special attention; and deliveries must be punctual. It's helpful if he's familiar with the church or reception site, because he will be aware of lighting problems and the layout of the area. If he is unfamiliar with the wedding site, be sure he checks the place well in advance of your wedding.

If all details, including the price, are agreeable, confirm all arrangements with the florist in writing by letter or memo.

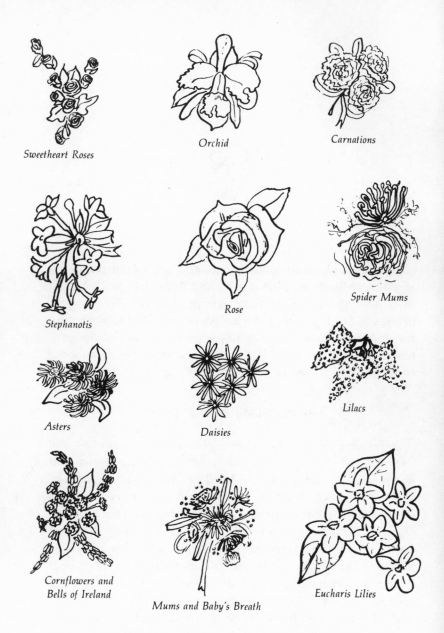

Sweetheart Roses

Orchid

Carnations

Stephanotis

Rose

Spider Mums

Asters

Daisies

Lilacs

Cornflowers and
Bells of Ireland

Mums and Baby's Breath

Eucharis Lilies

FLOWERS COMMONLY USED IN WEDDINGS

The florist may require a deposit, but under no circumstances should the total be paid before the day of your wedding. On your wedding day, appoint someone to check that the flowers received are correct, delivered on time, and arranged properly.

NONPROFESSIONAL HELP

Couples who live in warm climates where flowers grow year round or who live in the northern half of the United States during the spring or summer months may consider decorating artistically with fresh-cut flowers or flowering shrubs gathered from a country garden. With a little bit of luck, a member of your local garden club may offer help. Or a neighbor or friend whose passion is gardening will be a marvelous source of information.

The order for flowers from your florist for the bridal bouquet and corsages may be combined with decorating the church and/or the reception site. If you can find a friend or relative to tastefully arrange table centerpieces at the reception, this can cut costs enormously. Other economical tips are to designate someone to unobtrusively transport the flowers from the church to the reception site and to have the bridesmaids place their flowers in a designated flower holder on the bridal table. This relieves them of the responsibility of finding a place to put them, and it also enhances the appearance of the table.

FLOWERS IN CHURCH

There may be some regulations regarding use of floral decorations in your church, so it's vital that you first check with your clergymember, or whoever is in charge of arrangements, before making any decisions.

Next, consider the lighting. Will it be a daytime or night-time wedding? If the church interior is dark, light shades of flowers are most effective. It's best to focus your attention on the altar. Here, a few well-placed potted plants or in-dividual flower arrangements often will do. Generally speaking, a large church with a high ceiling needs tall flower arrangements and more of them to give any impact at all. Even in a small church, flowers will be seen from a distance, therefore bold arrangements show up better than delicate small blossoms.

At an elaborate wedding, flowers or ribbons are draped down the aisle to mark the pews to indicate reserved seats for family members. Other options are to have greens or flowering sprays at strategic points or to use only greens with candles in the church windows for an evening wedding.

Finally, you may wish to add a large welcoming arrange-ment at the entrance or foyer of the church, but this is not vital. Remember when the bridesmaids in their colorful dresses walk down the aisle carrying lovely bouquets, all eyes are focused on them. It's a far better choice to decorate the reception site with flowers and table centerpieces than filling the church with massive flower arrangements. More time is spent at the reception, and flowers add a great deal of atmosphere to the liveliness and fun.

FOR A VERY SMALL WEDDING

It's a challenge to hold a small wedding in a large church, yet there are ways to overcome the feeling of emptiness by using the choir stalls in the chancel for seating guests and lighting only this section of the church. One may also define the perimeter with a hedge of potted plants or a row of greenery.

THE AISLE RUNNER

White runners are usually available through your florist. However, some people feel they are not necessary except on grass, but this is purely a personal decision. For example, at past White House weddings, aisle runners were not used because it was felt the gowns photographed better without them.

FLOWERS IN A PRIVATE SETTING—INDOORS

At a home, in a club, or at a hotel, a room with a fireplace creates an ideal setting for the ceremony. A fireplace may be filled with greens or plants, or the mantel may be decorated with green roping or an arrangement of flowers. Most florists and rental stores have stands available for flowers, potted plants, or candles, as well as arches, stanchions, and kneelers or prie-dieu.

A bay window is also a lovely setting for the ceremony, but one must be sure there is no glare during the time of the ceremony, otherwise the bridal couple will be mere silhouettes to the guests. If there is no fireplace or bay window, a screen or backdrop of greens may be placed against a wall as a backdrop for the ceremony. In the evening, draperies that are closed make a soft, attractive background for the ceremony.

The *chupah* is a flowered wedding bower placed over the altar in Jewish ceremonies. It symbolizes the home the couple will share and must be large enough to cover the rabbi and the immediate wedding party.

Flowers also make a lovely background for photographs. When posing for pictures, be sure to give some thought to the background, as many a good shot has been spoiled when taken in front of an open kitchen door or a view of the parking lot.

143

FLOWERS IN A PRIVATE SETTING—OUTDOORS

When the ceremony takes place in a garden, on a patio, under a tent, or by a pool, one can create many beauty spots to enhance the setting.

For added color, potted plants may be placed among the flower beds or greenery or on the patio. Or flowers may be floated in the pool. And, of course, arches decorated with flowers or standards may be placed in a designated area where the ceremony will be held. Even under a tent, branches or flowering twigs may be attached under the tenting to the posts for a dramatic effect. A friendly florist may be asked if he'd consider renting out potted plants for a few hours.

OTHER OUTDOOR DECORATIONS

Silver or gold helium-filled balloons with the name of the bridal couple and the date make sensational centerpieces or accents for an outdoor wedding. A cluster of balloons may be tied with colorful ribbons to enhance the lively effect.

THE BRIDAL BOUQUET

As the bride walks down the aisle, the head-to-toe effect of her outfit is accented by the flowers she carries. For example, if the gown has intricate detail in front, it's best to choose a single flower, but if the gown has simple lines in front with more design in the back, then one may prefer a more elaborate bouquet. Be sure to give the florist all the helpful information available about the bride's gown and the dresses of every member of the wedding party. With an old-fashioned wedding gown, the florist may recommend an old-fashioned or Victorian bouquet, probably one including

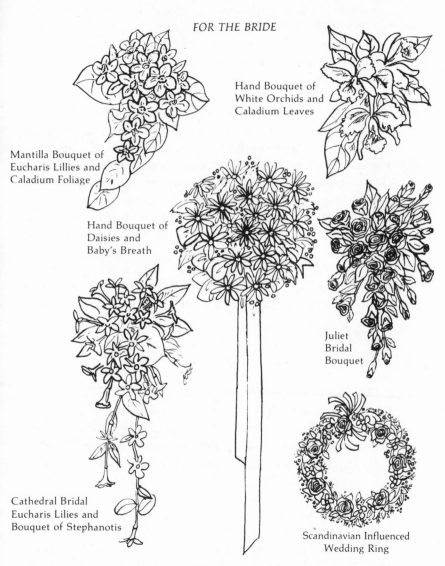

FOR THE BRIDE

Hand Bouquet of
White Orchids and
Caladium Leaves

Mantilla Bouquet of
Eucharis Lillies and
Caladium Foliage

Hand Bouquet of
Daisies and
Baby's Breath

Juliet
Bridal
Bouquet

Cathedral Bridal
Eucharis Lillies and
Bouquet of Stephanotis

Scandinavian Influenced
Wedding Ring

BRIDAL BOUQUETS
WITH FLOWERS FREQUENTLY USED

145

sweetheart roses, cornflowers, miniature carnations, and baby's breath. Or he may suggest a dried or silk arrangement with a lace collar. In some cases the bride may wish to carry a small family bible or a satin purse with a flower pinned to it.

For a very formal wedding, when the bride wears a long gown, she may choose a cascade arrangement of all-white flowers, such as white orchids, gardenias or camellias, stephanotis, and lilies of the valley. The bouquet may be made up of a single variety of flowers or a combination of several. Another option for the tall bride is an arrangement of calla lilies. Smaller brides will prefer more delicate arrangements. Also consider the texture of the gown when choosing your flowers. Eyelet and cotton are best complemented by daisies and violets. Camellias and gardenias, with their shiny dark leaves, are beautiful against a satin or brocade dress.

Surprisingly enough, attendants' flowers are often more eye-catching than the bridal bouquet, because it is the bride's dress, and not her flowers, that are the main focus of attention.

BRIDESMAIDS' FLOWERS

The flowers carried by the bridesmaids should be coordinated with the bride's bouquet. They may carry baskets of flowers filled with a multicolored spring arrangement; they may carry a nosegay or a long-stemmed arrangement of roses or chrysanthemums tied with a bow and held gracefully in the arms. They may carry a dried arrangement or fresh greens mixed with a few garden variety flowers. Bridesmaids sometimes carry a muff fashioned from flowers or from fur with a flower accent; with a Victorian-style dress, fans or parasols are a good choice. In short, just about anything the bride might select is suitable to carry out the theme of her wedding. One lovely wedding we attended

BRIDESMAID'S FLOWERS

147

took place in Hawaii where everyone in the wedding party wore flower leis.

HEADDRESSES

Brides, bridesmaids, and flower girls sometimes wear flowers as headdresses. (Austrian brides wear a wreath of fresh myrtle, which is considered a symbol of love.) Flowers formed into a crown or a tiara may be used with the wedding veil itself, or a combination of orange blossoms and ribbons is lovely. Flowers chosen for a headdress must look delicate but must also be sturdy enough to remain fresh and intact throughout the wedding.

MAID OR MATRON OF HONOR

The maid or matron of honor's bouquet is usually similar in style to the bridesmaids' bouquet but different in color. These distinctions help the guests to identify members of the wedding party.

THE GROOM, FATHERS, AND USHERS

Boutonnieres for the men consist of a single blossom, such as a carnation, rosebud, or shaft of lilies of the valley and are quite often white. The groom's boutonniere complements the bride's bouquet and is a little different from those of the ushers and fathers, whose boutonnieres are all alike.

THE FLOWER GIRL

The flower girl walks ahead of the bride and carries a nosegay or small basket decorated with flowers or ribbons.

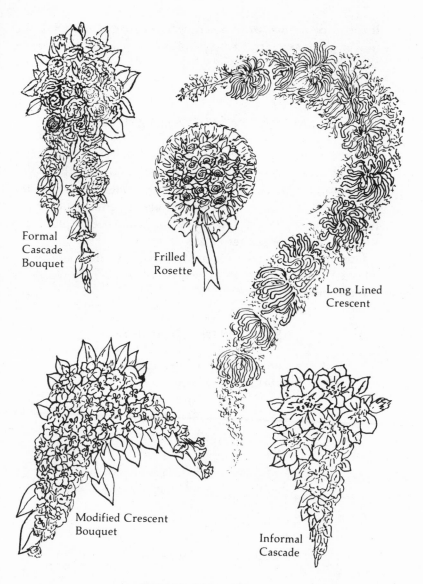

Formal
Cascade
Bouquet

Frilled
Rosette

Long Lined
Crescent

Modified Crescent
Bouquet

Informal
Cascade

FOR THE ATTENDANTS

149

If the bride wishes, and the church or synagogue allows, the flower girl may scatter rose petals in the path of the bride. A small headdress of flowers always looks adorable on little girls.

MOTHERS AND GRANDMOTHERS

Whoever is responsible for sending flowers may consider sending a corsage or a single flower to the mothers and grandmothers of the wedding couple. Some women prefer not to wear a corsage. It is a good idea to check with them before ordering flowers, because they may prefer pinning a single flower to a pocketbook.

Flowers help guests to identify these special persons with whom they may wish to exchange a few friendly words at the reception.

FLOWERS OF THE MONTH

January	Carnation
February	Violet
March	Jonquil
April	Sweet Pea
May	Lily of the Valley
June	Rose
July	Larkspur
August	Gladiolus
September	Aster
October	Calendula
November	Chrysanthemum
December	Narcissus

CHAPTER 10

Music

Just as my fingers on these keys make music
So the selfsame sounds on my spirit make a music too.

WALLACE STEVENS

Selecting your own special music for your wedding can be a gratifying experience. After all, carefully selected music helps create the atmosphere that makes the wedding uniquely your own.

There are usually two distinct types of music played at weddings. First, there's the majestic or lilting music to be sung or played during the ceremony, and, secondly, there's the entertaining or lively music to be played at the reception. Sometimes two separate sets of musicians need to be engaged. At other times the musicians are versatile and able to play both kinds of music for the ceremony and the reception.

MUSIC FOR THE CEREMONY IN CHURCH

The variety of music and combination of instruments used today is unbelievable! No longer is organ music and a soloist the only choice, but any kind of string and horn instruments can be used effectively. Yes, there are still restrictions, which vary from church to church. It is important, therefore, that the selections and the instruments to be played, be discussed thoroughly on the first visit to the clergyman's office. Sometimes he will refer the bridal couple to the organist, choir master, or soloist to advise on the selections which may or may not be played during the ceremony.

For instance, the Eastern Orthodox churches allow only vocal music, and Quakers allow no music whatsoever.

The half hour prior to the ceremony is the time during which the mood is set. During this prelude, favorite music, popular or classical, is usually included as well as vocal or instrumental solos. A solo may be sung just after the mother of the bride is seated.

When selecting a soloist, it is advisable to have a professional or an experienced singer who will not panic. A soloist hired for the occasion is paid. If the soloist, or organist, as the case may be, is a relative or friend, the situation becomes a little tricky. You may offer to pay the soloist, and then let it be his or her decision to accept the offer or not. Sometimes a professional, who might charge a substantial fee, will give the gift of song to the bridal couple instead of a standard gift-wrapped wedding present. If the soloist is obviously a member of the wedding party, then a gift to him or her is appropriate.

After the prelude, the processional begins and the music at this time is joyful, dignified, and majestic, with a regular beat, so you'll feel comfortable walking slowly and in time with the music. When the wedding party reaches the altar, the bride walks down the aisle to music that announces her entrance. Sometimes music is played softly during the exchange of marriage vows, but this is a matter of individual choice and church rule. At the end of the ceremony, the recessional begins and this is triumphant and slightly quicker tempo than the processional. It might be fun to go to a record shop and ask to hear a record of wedding music and make your own personal selections. Most music stores also have books containing processionals and recessionals for weddings. Or an experienced musician who often plays at weddings may be used as a resource person to help set your mind at ease.

MUSIC FOR THE CEREMONY IN A PRIVATE SETTING

There are, of course, no restrictions but your own good taste when it comes to music in your home, club, or social hall. A pianist or a soloist or a guitarist or a trio of any kind always help to set the mood—and so do records! When hiring musicians be sure to discuss what they will be wearing. You will want the musicians' dress to blend correctly with the tone of your wedding. Also allow plenty of set-up time for instruments. It's better to have them waiting for you than you to be waiting for them! And finally, sign a written contract, probably with a down payment, and arrange for final payment in cash or by check when they are through playing.

MUSIC FOR THE RECEPTION

Music is crucial to setting the mood at your reception. Decide what kind of mood you want to create, and then find the musicians to create it. Your personal preference, whether you choose light classical pieces or current popular songs, is your best choice. It is helpful if you give the musicians a list of songs to play and enough time to learn the music. Also, warn the band if Uncle Joe is apt to get up and play the saxophone during the reception. It will be much easier on the band leader to be forewarned. Music serves as a pleasant background while guests pass through the receiving line, and if there's dancing afterwards, music becomes the glue that holds the party together. For people who enjoy good conversation and food more than dancing, a classical string quartet may create an interesting baroque effect. If you cannot audition the musicians live, most professional groups or individuals have tapes you can listen to before you engage them. They will probably want to check the size of the room and the acoustics so they will select the right instruments.

RECORDING THE CEREMONY ON TAPE

"Oh, I wish we had taped the music," is a feeling that is often expressed after the wedding. During the ceremony, because of the high emotional level, the couple may not actually hear the music played. Therefore, taping the music and the service is worth considering for future enjoyment. It is also particularly nice in case an older member of the family cannot attend or to play back for someone who has been far away.

WHERE TO FIND YOUR MUSICIANS

For a church wedding, your minister will be able to help you. When the wedding or reception takes place at home, in a private club or hall, in a hotel, or any private room and you are not familiar with local musicians, check the Yellow Pages of the telephone book for listings of local music teachers' associations or the musicians' union. Other good sources are the music department of a local college or university. Music stores usually have a list of names to recommend.

SETTING FEES

Musicians usually set their own fees according to their ability and experience, and it's good to remember that their time involved should be taken into consideration. If the musicians are going to be present at the rehearsal, and if they need time to practice special music or rehearse with other instrumentalists, the charge is more, naturally.

Musicians will expect to take a break during the reception and be given something to eat and drink. This matter should be discussed early during negotiations.

SUGGESTED WEDDING MUSIC

Prelude Music

Choose one or two favorite songs to set the mood. Combine these with traditional selections which include classical as well as popular tunes. We suggest, "Theme from Romeo and Juliet" by Tchaikovsky or the contemporary arrangement by Nino Rota. A vocal selection, such as "Sunrise, Sunset" from *Fiddler on the Roof* may be sung while parents and grandparents are being seated.

Processional Music

A traditional majestic march played for the wedding party as they proceed down the aisle helps carry the spirit of all those present to the altar. Two favorite compositions are, "Wedding March" by Alexander Guilmant and "Marche Nuptiale" by Allan Caron. The familiar bridal chorus from *Lohengrin* by Wagner, as well as the recessional "Wedding March" from *A Midsummer Night's Dream* by Mendelssohn were at one time considered inappropriate to be played in church, because of the pagan nature of the drama. However, since Vatican II any restrictions have been lifted from these popular melodies, and they are played regularly at many weddings.

Wedding Ceremony Music

Selections played or sung during the ceremony are extremely variable depending solely on the couple's preferences. Popular classical examples are "Ich liebe dich" by Grieg and "The Lord's Prayer" by Malotte. A current favorite that is frequently sung is the "Wedding Song," published by Warner Brothers.

Recessional Music

The joyful spirit of the recessional music carries the wedding party up the aisle after the ceremony. Classical music selections often played are the "Wedding March" from *A Midsummer Night's Dream* by Mendelssohn and "Trumpet Voluntary in D" by Purcell.

Reception Music

Any sentimental favorite that cannot be included in the wedding ceremony may be played during the reception. Some examples are "Endless Love" by Lionel Richie, "Longer" by Daniel Fogelberg, and "Feelings" by Morris Albert.

Second Wedding Music

Selections for prelude and wedding ceremony music are the same as those played at a first wedding. There are common vocal solos that are sentimental favorites of all those caught up in the beauty and romance of love. The main differences lie in the selection of processional and recessional music. In second weddings, choices lean toward nontraditional and lighter selections such as the "Westminster Abbey Hymn" by Purcell or "Jesu, Joy of Man's Desiring" by Bach for the processional, or the theme from "Water Music" by Handel for a recessional.

CHAPTER 11

Photographs

Above all, I craved to seize the whole essence, in the confines of one single photograph of some situation that was in the process of unrolling itself before my eyes.

HENRI CARTIER-BRESSON

CHOOSING A PHOTOGRAPHER

The best way to choose a photographer is to visit his studio, carefully look over sample albums, and discuss your photographic budget openly.

There's just one more thing. I strongly recommend choosing an experienced, professional wedding photographer over a good portrait photographer. There are so many social touches an experienced wedding photographer has been trained to do that will please you. For instance, he or she must know how to dress for a wedding. You'd hardly want someone showing up in a T-shirt and jeans; yet this can happen! Or having someone barge into the refreshment line ahead of your guests, which has happened, also.

Many a bride has been unnecessarily upset by an overbearing and demanding photographer. Pictures are important—there's no second chance—and a photographer who has been trained and specializes in weddings can be a joy, not only on this momentous day, but the results of his efforts will be treasured for a lifetime. Long after the flowers have wilted, the cake has been eaten, the guests have returned home, the only concrete lifetime evidence for all your efforts lies in the photographic recording of your wedding day!

Your wedding pictures may be in black and white, which is less expensive, or in color. During the interview, find out how many proofs he will take. Some photographers take the pictures and provide prints as part of their service. Others only take pictures and give the negatives to the couple to have printed. The latter method is less expensive.

Most photographers ask for a deposit when they take an assignment and expect full payment upon delivery of the photographs. How much of a deposit is required? How much will it cost you or the members of the wedding party to have duplicate photos made up? There should be a reduction in price for ordering photos in quantity.

The bride usually presents a formal wedding photograph, or an enlarged candid, to the parents of the groom. She may furnish appropriate pictures to any friends or relatives. If the groom's family desires any additional pictures, it is best to offer to pay for them in a businesslike way. Wedding pictures also are a thoughtful thank-you gift to the attendants.

Most important, who will the actual photographer be? Will it be the owner of the studio or one of his assistants? Again, confirm all arrangements in writing. Just remember, to photograph a wedding from beginning through the reception may take as much as eight hours of the photographer's time.

POSSIBLE PHOTOGRAPHS

- Formal engagement portrait—optional
- Formal wedding portrait in wedding gown and suit taken of the couple at the studio prior to the wedding for newspaper release. These studio photos are far superior than any candids taken on the day of the wedding

- Pictures taken at home before the wedding are optional
- Pictures taken at the church or during the ceremony
- Pictures taken at the reception may be formal pictures of the bride and groom alone, with the bridesmaids, and with the entire wedding party. These are followed by photographs of the couple with each set of parents and, if they wish, with other members of the immediate family. In case of divorced parents, each one usually has the picture taken with the couple separately. Stepparents are included, if they are on close terms with the bride and groom.
- Candid pictures only, or in addition to the formal pictures, may be taken at the reception. These candids might include pictures of guests, the bridal couple cutting the cake, and the bride throwing the bouquet.

For candid photographs at the reception, it's necessary to provide the photographer with a written list of special people you want photographed. You might say, "Please be sure to take a picture of my grandparents with the mayor." Then designate someone to point these people out to him.

PICTURES IN THE CHURCH

Most churches have some restrictions regarding photographs taken during the wedding ceremony. Beautiful photographs may be taken with today's film without a flash bulb, using available light only. The photographer should be as inconspicuous as possible throughout the procession and the ceremony. Ushers should ask wedding guests arriving with cameras to please refrain from taking flash pictures in the sanctuary. This may seriously interfere with the work of the professional photographer. It also greatly detracts from the solemnity of the occasion to have clicking and flashing during the ceremony.

PICTURES AT THE RECEPTION

Instead of keeping guests waiting outside a reception site while the bridal party is having formal pictures taken after the ceremony, many people prefer taking pictures after all the guests have passed through the receiving line at the reception. Again, guests should not interfere with the work of the professional photographer by taking flash pictures until he is finished.

AMATEUR PHOTOGRAPHERS

Sometimes a friend will offer to take your wedding pictures, but don't trust your once-in-a-lifetime memories to a once-in-a-while photographer! This may be risky for all the afore-mentioned reasons. I would graciously decline having my friend take wedding pictures. As a guest at your wedding, the friend may be off somewhere having a good time (and isn't that the reason he was invited?) just when you wish he would be there for the cake cutting or whatever. Instead, suggest that he or she take some extra candids before the wedding or at the reception. Or suggest taking movies as a permanent record of the day.

VIDEO TAPE

There are two good reasons to consider having the wedding video taped: it will be fun to play the tape back, just for your own pleasure. And it may also be shown to a close member of the family, who for various reasons, was unable to attend the ceremony. It is possible to rent video-tape machines by the day. There are also professional wedding photographers who will handle video taping for you.

NEWSPAPERS

Check with the society editor of your local newspaper as to their photographic requirements. Generally, newspapers ask for an 8-by-10-inch black and white glossy print. Most papers have a form to be filled out with the necessary information for an article to go with the picture.

MAKEUP

One way you can help the photographer take beautiful pictures of your wedding is by applying makeup properly. No makeup at all makes your picture appear washed out and anemic. Too much makeup, such as heavy false eyelashes, will cast unwanted shadows on your eyes. Ideally, makeup should look natural. Some brides engage a professional makeup artist to "do" the entire wedding party or the bride and her attendants. Here are some helpful hints from international makeup expert Glenna Franklin:

1. It is not necessary to buy expensive products. Most department stores or drug stores have adequate supplies, or your own favorite makeup may be used.
2. Choose a makeup close to your skin tone. If the foundation is too dark it will create a masklike effect.
3. Apply a concealer with a sponge to cover circles under the eyes or blemishes. Apply foundation smoothly into the hair line. Cover face and neck with a fine powder and blend well with a brush. Avoid a shiny skin because the camera may produce a highlight that is almost impossible to remove.
4. Use soft brown pencil for liner on eyes. Apply brown powder using a sponge tipped applicator on top of pencil to set liner and avoid smearing.

THE COMPLETE WEDDING PLANNER

5. Use black or brown mascara. Do not use a pale or frosted eyeliner or shadow.

6. Keep the shape of your eyebrows natural, and color brows lightly with a soft, gentle stroke.

7. Apply a touch of rouge or blush high on your cheekbones and blend carefully.

8. Use a lipliner pencil and draw the natural lip line. (This helps prevent lipstick from running.) Blend with a cotton swab and cover with pastel lipstick. Add a touch of gloss in center of lower lip.

Even though the bride and groom always wear eyeglasses and may feel they are a part of them, I recommend not wearing glasses in formal photographs for the following reasons: glasses reflect highlights that detract from a photograph (it is possible to remove the lenses from the frame for studio portraits); styles in glasses change, and this dates a picture; glasses hide facial features and family resemblances such as brows, the bridge of a nose, and eyes.

CHAPTER 12

Gift Registry

The great secret of successful marriage is to treat all disasters as incidents and none of the incidents as disasters.

HAROLD NICHOLSON

THE ADVANTAGES

Gift registering is a free service given by department stores, jewelry stores, and gift shops which offers only advantages and no disadvantages! These advantages appeal to the bride and groom, to the shopper, and to the store itself.

The advantage to the bride and groom is that both can share the fun of registering together, of choosing gifts they will be delighted to receive, and having something they can enjoy using for years to come. They may choose the exact colors and designs that fit their decor; the right china patterns that harmonize with their selection of silverware and glassware; and they can cut down enormously on the precious hours it might take to return and exchange three identical toasters, six hideous orange bath towels, and a king-size blanket for a queen-size bed.

The advantage to the shopper is time saved when selecting a present that is sure to be well received and that is within the price range. Registering eliminates all doubts and uncertainty.

The advantage to the store is that registering cuts down on returns and exchanges, which are costly procedures. And because registering brings additional business to the department stores and gift shops, the service of bridal consultants is provided to help couples in making their selections.

The bridal consultant fills out a form and records patterns and color choices for tableware, linens, kitchen accessories, and so forth. Some stores display a special table with the bride's name on a little card, along with her selection of china, silver, and glass patterns.

Registering may be a boon when you make an appointment with an experienced consultant in one of the better shops or in the main branch of a department store that has a wide selection. The system can completely fail if you drop in at a branch store where a part-time, so-called bridal consultant without any training or experience is on duty. Again, my suggestion is to shop around until you do find the right person to advise you. They are out there!

And this is the hardheaded advice you'll hear from them: "Take your time in making your selections. Come back and look around again. China, silver, and glassware costs a lot of money, and you have to live with it for a long time. Don't choose hastily."

Some bridal consultants are quite knowledgeable in pointing out, for example, the different characteristics of bone china, stoneware, iron ware and earthenware. He or she knows which patterns are "open stock" and will explain the pluses and minuses of new materials. Even when people know what they like, it's smart to listen to what the consultant has to say.

Usually a couple chooses the china pattern first and builds around that. For years, consultants have been encouraging people to select all-white chinaware. Yes, it's stark and dramatic in its simplicity and goes with everything, but the other side of the coin in favor of patterns is that a whole room's decor can be built around a spectacular chinaware design, and the results may be equally dramatic and quite original. In addition, I always choose a china pattern with an attractive, colorful border, because the food on the plate is automatically garnished and looks more appetizing. If we stop and think about this for a moment, we realize that many delicious foods we enjoy eating don't have great eye appeal because they lack color. Take items like mashed potatoes, cauliflower, noodles and rice, which are all white, and to this we add other pale foods, such as chicken and fish or meats, which are usually brown. To make an attractive presentation, we need to add colorful vegetables and garnishes, particularly when using a solid white plate.

It must be remembered that, even though a couple is registered, this does not mean they will receive a complete set of anything. Whatever they do get, it's a start, and usually members of the family are delighted to add to the collection on birthdays and anniversaries.

Admittedly, it can become very confusing when confronted with hundreds of patterns for china, linens, flatware, and all the other accessories. My advice to every young couple is to try and think about the way you like to dress. Most people know if they are the tailored type or the casual type; sporty or sophisticated; arty or ethnic; muted or bold type. Once your clothing preference is pinpointed, you may readily translate clothing preferences and colors into home-decorating selections with good, positive results.

Before registering for a lot of odds and ends, it's good to think somewhat about your probable future lifestyle. Do you both come from large families and will there be a lot of casual or formal entertaining? If so, then concentrate on a complete set of chinaware, flatware, and glassware. Do you adore cooking? If so, register for a slew of time-saving kitchen appliances. Do your jobs demand a lot of travel? Then you may prefer choosing sturdy lifetime luggage. Do you expect to inherit some treasured heirlooms? Then choose designs that will be compatible.

When registering, select a wide price range from which friends and relatives can make choices. It's possible that two or three friends may wish to purchase one important piece for you. Or someone will look for a simple shower gift or combine two items instead of one.

It's perfectly all right to be registered for bedroom and bathroom linens in one store and for china, silver, and glassware in another store.

There is an advantage to registering with a national chain department store when families are scattered all over the country. The bride's gift selection will only be forwarded, however, to another store at the request of the shopper. It does not automatically go to each store all over the country. For this and other reasons it pays to call by phone and check that the service is working after registering.

THE SECOND TIME AROUND

Should people getting married again register also? Of course they should! This service can be a real boon not only to couples who have accumulated a mixture of "his" and "her" furnishings but can be helpful to all their friends and relatives.

Registering for wedding gifts may help fill gaps that appear over the years in the most complete households. Are the old monogrammed towels getting frayed? Are there nine red-wine glasses, four white-wine glasses, and three on-the-rocks glasses in the cupboard? Or what about a modern kitchen accessory? A well-chosen gift is just as appreciated by any couple the second time around.

SHARING THE PLEASURE

It is especially thoughtful and much appreciated by the groom's family when the bride or groom takes a moment to inform them of the gifts that have been sent by friends of the groom's family. A simple list may be telephoned or mailed to the groom's parents from time to time, both before and after the wedding. Then when they meet their friends or business acquaintances, they may have the pleasure of telling them that the gift was received and enjoyed by their son and future daughter-in-law. It's a good way to build bridges between the two families.

DISPLAYING GIFTS

There are some families who follow the charming custom of displaying wedding gifts at the bride's home. Sometimes a special day is set aside for friends and relatives to visit and share in a few light refreshments. Or, if the reception is at the bride's parents' home, then this is an opportune time to decorate a long table where gifts are displayed attractively for everyone to admire. Beside each gift is the donor's card, but checks are kept in envelopes and are not displayed.

The advantage of this custom is to permit close relatives of the groom and everyone's friends to "oh and ah" over all the gifts at one time.

The disadvantage is that this custom takes a good deal of time and space, along with a tremendous amount of tact to arrange three blenders and five pairs of candlesticks so that people won't notice duplications. And finally, the gifts can't be exchanged until after the honeymoon.

Instead of displaying gifts before the wedding, it may be more convenient to invite friends to the couple's home after the wedding where they may have the pleasure of seeing the gifts in their proper setting.

Whatever the approach, it really doesn't make any important difference—it's mostly a matter of space, convenience, and local custom.

BROKEN GIFTS

When a gift arrives broken, the first thing to do is to determine if the package was sent from a store, in which case the gift is insured and will be replaced by the store. If the gift was delivered by UPS, a claim is filed with this agency, but the gift must remain in the original carton for inspection. If the gift was mailed through the U.S. mail and was insured, it is necessary to take the damaged gift in the original package to the post office to process the claim.

In case a gift arrives broken but is not insured, it is best to write a thank-you note without mentioning the mishap.

MISSING GIFT CARDS

Occasionally a store will slipup and omit the gift card. In case this happens, notify the store, and they will trace the sale and inform you who the donor is.

MONOGRAMMING

When Anne Jennifer Lovejoy marries Robert William Baldwin the linen monogram may be done with the letter "B" in the center and the bride's first name and surname on either side of the "B" in smaller letters.

Or if the letters are all the same size, the monogram may read:

If one initial is used it may be the letter "B."

There are many ways to engrave silver, and most jewelers are able to help make choices. When a single letter is used it may be the first letter or either the bride's or groom's surname. When three letters are used, it may be the same as above or it may be the initial of both the bride and groom's first names centered above or below the initial of their surname.

CHAPTER 13

Transportation

What is not good for the hive
is not good for the bee.

MARCUS AURELIUS

When people say, "What can I do to help?" here's the perfect assignment for someone who likes to organize! Arranging for reliable transportation is an important duty to perform for the bridal couple. This includes transportation from home to the site of the ceremony and from there to the reception for all members of the wedding party.

First, you have to know the number of people that need transportation in order to estimate the number of cars required. The parking situation needs to be carefully evaluated at all three locations—at the home, at the site of the ceremony, and at the reception. If there is a traffic problem, the police may be notified and they will send an officer to survey the parking or to handle any traffic bottleneck.

In some cases it's necessary to provide maps for out-of-town guests or to some of the volunteer drivers. Maps may be sketched by hand or the original may be reprinted on a duplicating machine with names and places indicated thereon. Talking about maps and directions, I'm reminded of the note author Robert Louis Stevenson sent to his friend James Barrie inviting him to come and visit on Samoa, an island in the South Pacific. "You take the boat at San Francisco, then my place is the second to the left." Most directions are not this simple, and a good map will keep people from getting lost or being delayed.

WHO GOES FIRST

At a traditional formal wedding, the bride's mother, along with several bridesmaids, leaves the house first in one car and is followed by the rest of the attendants in as many cars as are necessary. The last car transports the bride and her father to the ceremony.

When the reception is held away from church, transportation also needs to be arranged in advance. The bride and groom are the first to leave for the reception, followed by both sets of parents and the bride's attendants.

TRANSPORTATION CHOICES

To add spice to the trip, the bride and groom may enjoy riding to the reception in an open convertible, an antique car, a horse and buggy or a sleigh, depending of course on the locale and time of year.

Finally, hiring limousines is a desirable option for a formal wedding. The advantage is that these cars are spacious, clean, and it's relaxing to sit back and be transported by a competent uniformed driver. In urban communities rental limousine services may be found in the yellow section of the phone book. In small, rural communities, the local funeral director will put you in touch with chauffeurs for hire.

PARKING AT THE CEREMONY AND RECEPTION

When the wedding is large and parking is at a premium, it is thoughtful to provide attendants to park cars. In small communities, it may be possible to engage high-school students or athletic teams who will channel the profit toward a school project. In large cities there are parking services available that will park guests' cars as they arrive and return the cars to them when they leave.

CHAPTER 14

The Rehearsal

To be prepared is half the victory.

CERVANTES

THE NEED FOR A REHEARSAL

For an informal home wedding of twenty-five or more guests or for a cathedral wedding of hundreds, a rehearsal is the best insurance for a perfect performance on this meaningful day.

Without a rehearsal, timing is off. People are bumping into each other or turning the wrong way, exits and entrances are awkward, and everyone is nervous and uneasy. The spiritual beauty of the wedding is enhanced when all these little problems are worked out neatly in advance.

The people required to attend the rehearsal are the clergymember, judge or stand-in, the bride and groom, their parents, all the attendants, the musicians and/or soloist.

Often the clergymember will choose to speak to the bridal couple during the rehearsal about the religious meaning of the wedding ceremony. This exercise helps to relieve tension and puts the couple more at ease.

The rehearsal should be held where the wedding will take place in order to practice the processional, recessional, the entrances and exits. It is important for the wedding party to know how long it takes to get from one place to another, and the musicians need to be cued when to start singing or playing.

If the ceremony is performed in a church that has no center aisle but two main aisles, one aisle may be ignored. Another option is to have the processional go down one aisle and the recessional go up the other aisle. This decision depends on whether the church will be completely filled or not.

When both aisles are used, the parents are seated in the front row of the center pew—the bride's parents on the left and groom's parents on the right. If only one aisle is being used for the processional and recessional, the parents are seated on either side of the aisle.

When the wedding is held in a church, some ministers or sextons prefer to be in complete charge of the rehearsal, as they are familiar with the church and have preferences as to how they like things done. If the clergymember is not interested in all the details, someone knowledgeable, such as a wedding coordinator, may direct the rehearsal.

THE REHEARSAL

The rehearsal will proceed smoothly and take far less time if one person is in charge, otherwise there may be unnecessary, long discussions and differences of opinion. As soon as the wedding party is assembled, people should be placed exactly where they will be standing during the ceremony. The clergymember faces the bride and groom, with attendants on both sides of the couple. After everyone knows exactly where he or she is going to be, then they can begin practicing how to get there.

The Processional

The groom and the best man enter from a side room on signal from the clergymember and await the bride's entrance at the altar. The ushers proceed down the aisle first, in pairs and according to height, the shorter ones preceding the taller ones. Next come the bridesmaids, in pairs and according to height. The maid or matron of honor follows alone. If there is a flower girl, she precedes the bride, and the ring bearer precedes the flower girl. If there are any pages, they follow the bride and carry her train.

The bride may walk down the aisle alone, with her mother, or on her father's (or male relative's) arm. The right or left arm depends on the clergymember's preference. Most people prefer using the right arm because it is more graceful for the father to seat himself in the left front pew without crossing over the bride's train.

The processional walk is one of the most enjoyable highlights of the wedding for the guests. Watching the processional slowly moving down the aisle and observing the handsome ushers, the smiling bridesmaids in their lovely gowns, the ever-radiant bride in her beautiful costume, enjoying the flowers and listening to the couples' favorite musical selections, all this combines to provide a tender moment in the wedding proceedings. To savor this enchanting moment to the utmost, it is essential that the ushers pace their steps very slowly, starting left foot first, down the aisle, and keeping four pews apart. Usually this takes a bit of practice as most young men are anxious to tear down the aisle, but it is well worth the extra time devoted to this exercise. Ushers should walk erectly, but not stiffly, without swaying from side to side like sheaves in the wind. The attendants should look straight ahead, but if they happen to catch someone's eye, they may give a little smile of recognition.

The bride counts eight beats of the music or doubles the space between the attendants and follows the maid or matron of honor to the altar. The music stops playing when the bride reaches the chancel steps.

It is not necessary for small children to stand during the entire ceremony or take part in the recessional. They may instead be seated with their parents at a designated time.

The Ceremony Rehearsal

The clergymember usually instructs the couple regarding the ceremony, and they practice the exchange of marriage vows, the blessing of the rings, along with the kneeling and rising.

In most religious and civil ceremonies the custom of giving away the bride is optional. The father or a close male relative may respond to the question as to who gives away the bride with "I do" or, in some cases, "Her mother and I do" or "We do." If the father is too ill or infirm to walk down the aisle, he may still participate in the ceremony. He may be seated in a pew or in a wheelchair before the bride's mother is escorted down the aisle, or the mother may be stationed in her pew and nod, "I do" in response to the question of "Who gives this woman in holy matrimony?" An alternative to this question is a pledge by parents to support with love the two persons in their marriage relationships.

After the Ceremony

The groom has the honor to be the first man to kiss the bride, although at a large formal church wedding this is frequently not done.

At an informal or garden wedding, the clergymember may elect to introduce the newlyweds as Mr. and Mrs. to the assembled guests and the couple will remain where they are standing to receive the guests, without a recessional.

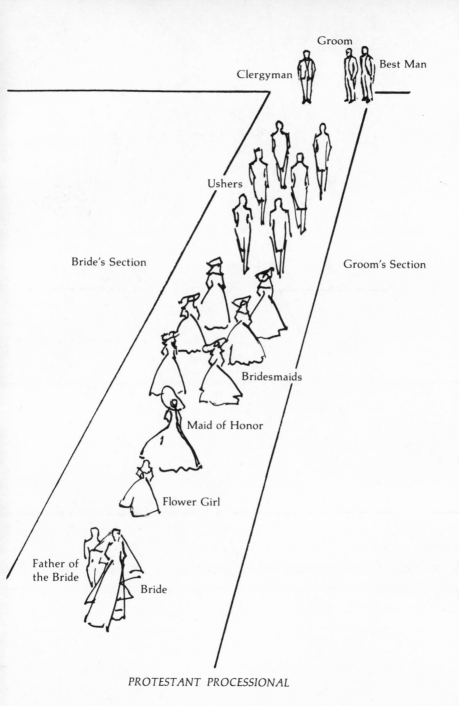

Groom

Clergyman

Best Man

Ushers

Bride's Section

Groom's Section

Bridesmaids

Maid of Honor

Flower Girl

Father of
the Bride

Bride

PROTESTANT PROCESSIONAL

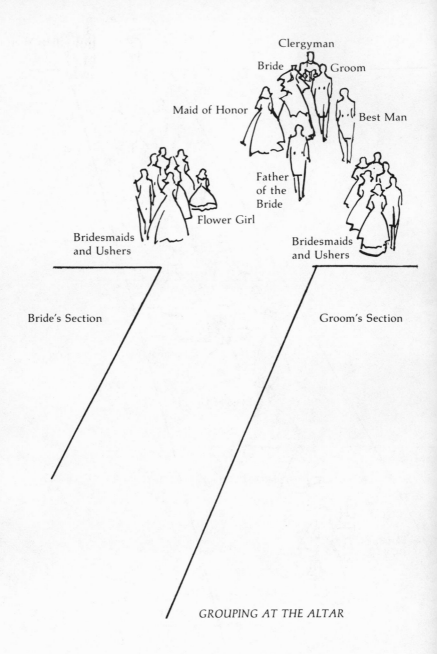

Clergyman

Bride   Groom

Maid of Honor   Best Man

Father
of the
Bride

Flower Girl

Bridesmaids   Bridesmaids
and Ushers   and Ushers

Bride's Section   Groom's Section

GROUPING AT THE ALTAR

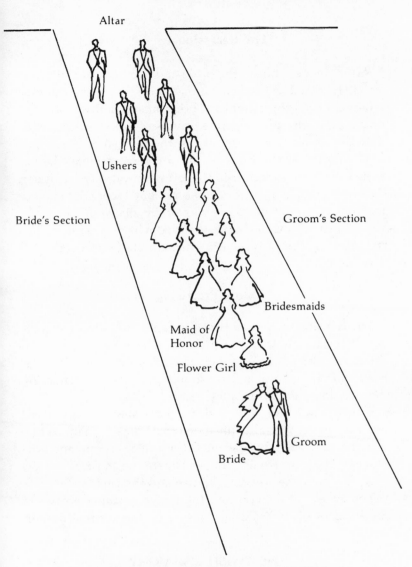

Altar

Ushers

Bride's Section

Groom's Section

Bridesmaids

Maid of
Honor

Flower Girl

Groom

Bride

PROTESTANT RECESSIONAL—TRADITIONAL
OPTIONAL ARRANGEMENT MAY BE USED (PAIRED)

The Recessional

After the ceremony, the bride and groom lead the recessional, followed by the maid or matron of honor. It is optional whether or not the ushers and bridesmaids pair up as couples or return in the two separate groups as in the processional. This decision depends entirely on the clergymember.

The father of the bride is not in the recessional—he has joined the bride's mother in the left pew and stays with her. The best man, as mentioned before, may escort the maid or matron of honor up the aisle, or he may not be in the recessional but instead meet the groom in the vestibule. The members of the congregation remain standing during the recessional.

More Practicing

The rehearsal is a good time for ushers to practice escorting the bride's mother and the groom's mother to and from their seats, or the bridesmaids may play the role of guests. For a church wedding, ushers should also practice dismissing the remaining guests pew by pew.

Before adjourning, the wedding party should be gathered together to go over any questions that remain unanswered.

If the clergymember permits, the bride, groom, and witnesses (who are usually the best man and maid of honor) may now sign the wedding license and the certificate.

The rehearsal is over, and the entire wedding party can relax and look forward with pleasure to the rehearsal dinner.

THE JEWISH CEREMONY

The Jewish religion has three distinct denominations—Orthodox or traditional; Conservative, which is less strict;

and Reform, which is the most lenient of all and has no laws regarding food.

There are many similarities among the three denominations and some small differences.

In Orthodox and Conservative synagogues, all men in the congregation must cover their heads as a sign of respect. There are skullcaps available in the vestibule for anyone who does not have a hat. Women usually also have their heads covered. Men and women do not sit together. In an Orthodox or Conservative ceremony, the bride's family sits on the right side and the groom's family sits on the left side of the aisle. Reform temples are reversed and the same as in Christian churches.

In Orthodox and Conservative weddings, the rabbi is waiting at the altar before the Holy Ark. He stands under a *chupah* or flowered bower, which symbolizes the home the couple will share.

The ushers walk down the aisle in pairs, followed by the bridesmaids also in pairs, followed by the best man who walks alone. Then comes the groom between his parents, his mother on the right and his father on the left, or as is more common today, the groom may be waiting at the altar with the best man. The maid of honor is next in the procession, followed by the flower girl, if any. Finally, the bride arrives between her parents, her mother on her right and father on her left. The bride stands to the groom's right. The wedding couple, the best man, and maid of honor stand under the *chupah* with the rabbi. If there is room, the fathers or both sets of parents are included. Otherwise they stand close by, each set of parents near their offspring. Grandparents may participate in the processional and ceremony under the *chupah* as well, if there is room.

In the Orthodox and Conservative service, at the close of the ceremony the bridegroom crushes a wineglass beneath

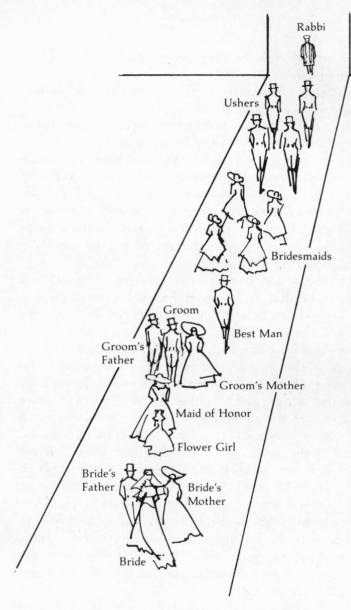

Rabbi

Ushers

Bridesmaids

Groom

Best Man

Groom's
Father

Groom's Mother

Maid of Honor

Flower Girl

Bride's
Father

Bride's
Mother

Bride

ORTHODOX OR CONSERVATIVE
JEWISH PROCESSIONAL

194

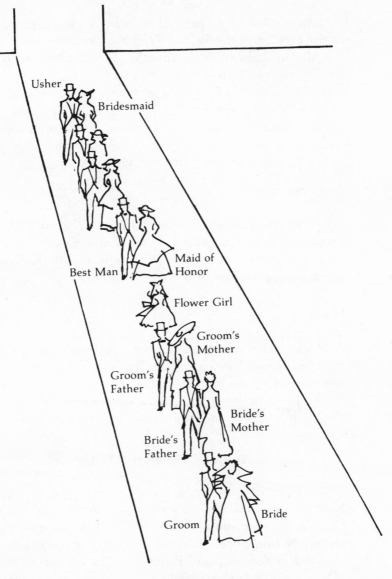

Usher
Bridesmaid

Best Man
Maid of
Honor

Flower Girl

Groom's
Mother

Groom's
Father

Bride's
Mother

Bride's
Father

Groom
Bride

ORTHODOX OR
CONSERVATIVE JEWISH RECESSIONAL

195

his foot making a loud noise. This reminds the congregation of the sacking of the Second Temple of Jerusalem in 70 A.D. It is also an old superstition that the glass breaking scares the devil's evil spirits away from the couple.

In the Reform wedding, the father escorts his daughter on his right arm down the aisle where the groom, his best man, and the rabbi are waiting at the altar. There is usually no canopy and no ceremonial glass is broken, though these may be optional in many Reform ceremonies.

The Recessional

In the Orthodox and Conservative services, the bride and groom go first, followed by the bride's parents and the groom's parents, followed by the attendants. In the Reform recessional, parents follow the attendants.

Music

At large Orthodox and Conservative weddings a cantor may be engaged to chant. At any of the weddings, the selection of music depends on the couple's own taste, with the advice of the music director. Instruments may vary from the organ in the Reform Temple to a violin, flute, or woodwinds.

EASTERN ORTHODOX WEDDINGS

The Holy Eastern Orthodox Catholic Apostolic Church has many ceremonial forms similar to the Roman Catholic Church but does not acknowledge the Pope as its spiritual leader. National traditions vary slightly according to the customs of the people of Russian, Slavic, or Greek origin. (The Greek Orthodox Wedding Ceremony has not changed since the ninth century.)

The ceremony always takes place during the daytime and in church. The bride's father gives her away at the altar and seats himself beside his wife. The procession is the same as in any other Christian service.

The Marriage Service is divided into two parts that follow in immediate succession: the preliminary Office of Betrothal and the Office of Crowning. At the Betrothal service the chief ceremony is the exchange and blessing of rings. This is an outward token that the two partners join in marriage of their own free will and consent. The second part of the service culminates in the ceremony of coronation. The priest places a crown on the heads of the bride and groom. Among the Greeks, the crowns are made of leaves and flowers, but among the Russians the crowns are of silver or gold. The crowns symbolize both joy and martyrdom, since every true marriage involves immeasurable self-sacrifice on both sides. At the end of the service, the couple drink from the same cup of wine, which recalls the miracle at the marriage feast of Cana in Galilee.

Music

The responses are usually sung by an acapella choir.

THE QUAKER CEREMONY

A Quaker wedding may take place either at home, in a garden, or in a meeting house. Usually there is no clergy-member to officiate at the wedding. The bride may or may not wear a wedding gown and veil.

On the wedding day, the bride and groom walk down the aisle together, or there may be the usual wedding procession. The couple take seats facing the meeting. After settling into a period of Quaker silence, people are moved by the spirit and may give a prayer or reflection and extend their good wishes to the couple. The couple then rise, hold hands, and exchange vows. After the couple sit down, the ushers bring a table with the Quaker marriage certificate. This is read aloud and signed by the bride, groom, overseers, and later officially registered. The ceremony is followed by the regular Quaker meeting. When the meeting is over all the members shake hands with those to the right and to the left. All guests sign the marriage certificate before leaving. The marriage certificate is treasured by the newlyweds as a memento of their wedding day.

Music

Some friends may have singing and music during the ceremony, but there generally are no alcoholic beverages at the reception.

THE CHRISTIAN SCIENCE CEREMONY

There is no ordained minister in the Christian Science church who has the authority to perform the marriage ceremony. Therefore when a member wishes to be married, a minister from any one of the Protestant faiths is invited to officiate. The couple may be married in the host church or at home. The ceremony is followed by a reception at which no alcoholic beverages are served. Otherwise a Christian Science wedding is similar to most Protestant weddings.

THE MORMON CEREMONY

The members of the Church of Jesus Christ of Latter-Day Saints practice two kinds of marriages. One ceremony is performed in the temple by the holy priesthood. The couple is declared wed "for time and for all eternity" instead of "until death do you part." All brides married in the temple dress in white and wear veils, even if they have been married before.

The second kind of marriage is a civil marriage performed by bishops of the Church or any other accredited person. If the couple complies with the requirements of the Church in their daily living, they may be married again in the temple of the Church for time and all eternity. Mormons abstain from drinking alcoholic beverages, and none are served at the reception, which is usually held in the cultural hall of the church or in the home of the bride's parents.

ECUMENICAL SERVICE

When the bride and groom belong to different faiths, it may be possible to hold the wedding in the bride or groom's church, home, or in a private room. A clergymember from each faith may coofficiate. One may read the vows, for example, and the other offer a blessing. In order to avoid having members of the clergy outpreach each other, it's best to make your feelings known tactfully in advance by discussing with both of them exactly who is going to say what during the ceremony.

THE CATHOLIC CEREMONY

Most Catholic weddings are centered around a nuptial mass which usually takes place in the afternoon or evening, but some Catholic weddings are performed without the Mass.

The processional, recessional, and most other details are similar to those described earlier in this chapter with the following differences.

THE COMPLETE WEDDING PLANNER

During the mass, the bride and groom are seated on two chairs before the altar, where there is a kneeling bench. The maid of honor and the best man remain in the sanctuary with the bride and groom. The attendants are sometimes seated in the front pews.

The bride and groom are the first to receive communion, followed by the ushers and bridesmaids and finally by the parents of the bride and groom. Then, any guests who wish to receive communion step up to the communion stations.

If the bride wishes, she may present a bouquet to the altar of the Blessed Virgin. The bride and groom together place the bouquet on the steps of the altar, usually accompanied by a short prayer.

In most Catholic churches, the priest introduces the newly-weds to the congregation, and in some, the guests respond with applause. The wedding party genuflect together and the recessional begins.

CHAPTER 15

On the Day of the Wedding

Marriage is that relation between man and woman in which independence is equal, the dependence is mutual, and the obligation is reciprocal.

LOUIS KAUFMAN ANSPACHER

Today the long-planned-for events fall neatly into place, hour by hour—starting with the delicious moment of awakening and ending the day for the bride and groom with a warm, cozy, new husband-and-wife relationship.

To enjoy every precious moment fully, it's a good idea to make up a final checklist outlining the whole day so that nothing is overlooked or forgotten. This list may be shared with the attendants.

ASSEMBLING THE WEDDING PARTY

At a home or garden wedding, getting everyone together is not very difficult, because the bride and her family are already there.

Providing a tray of tasty sandwiches is a thoughtful and most welcome touch. Often the members of the wedding party are too busy and excited to eat on the day of the wedding, and a little snack may prevent someone from having a sinking spell.

The bridesmaids may arrive either dressed or bring their gowns with them. They will offer to help the bride with any last-minute details of dressing. The makeup artist and hairdresser, if scheduled, arrive to complete their assignments. The florist has delivered the flowers, boutonnieres, and bouquets. The professional or amateur photographer takes candids at this time. Everyone admires the radiant bride and tells her how beautiful she looks, and she in turn, thanks everyone for being so kind, loving, and helpful.

In the meantime, the groom, his family and groomsmen may be gathering at his place and checking over their list of instructions until it is time to leave for the ceremony.

In the garden, the tent is in place; chairs are set up; flowers are arranged. Shrubs and bushes have been sprayed against flies, mosquitoes, and other insects. The caterer is in the kitchen preparing refreshments. The musicians are unpacking their instruments. The person who is performing the ceremony is looking over his notes. The guests are parking their cars and all systems are go!

ANOTHER WAY TO ASSEMBLE

When the ceremony takes place in a restaurant, club, or church, it may be more convenient to have everyone meet or dress, if space is provided, at the site of the ceremony. This depends on distance, transportation, the time of day, the number of people involved, and even the temperament of the bride and groom, who may prefer more privacy than hubbub.

THE CEREMONY IN A PRIVATE SETTING

There is very little difference between having a wedding ceremony at home, in a club, temple, synagogue, or in a church. I am going to describe the sequence of events of a

church wedding, knowing that the same procedure may be
followed in any other setting.

AT THE CHURCH

The ushers arrive forty-five minutes or an hour before
the ceremony and wait in the vestibule.

The groom and best man arrive about half an hour before
the ceremony, entering by a side door, where they wait in the
clergymember's study or the vestry until they receive the
signal that the ceremony is to begin.

Next the groom's parents and the bride's parents arrive at
the church and also wait in the vestibule.

SEATING THE BRIDE AND GROOM'S MOTHERS

When the bridesmaids are assembled, the groom's mother
is escorted to the front pew on the right by an usher. Her
husband follows right behind them. The last person escorted
to the front pew on the left is the mother of the bride. If any
guests arrive after she is already seated, they may unobtrusively slip into a back pew.

SEATING DIVORCED PARENTS

In case the bride or groom's parents are divorced and
remarried and everyone is on friendly terms, there are few
complications. The bride's mother and stepfather are seated
in the front pew on the left side of the aisle. Sometimes
when the family is large, other family members sit immediately behind them. Then the bride's father sits in the next
pew with his present wife and family. The same seating

arrangements hold for the groom's parents on the right side of the aisle.

When divorced parents are not on friendly terms, seating and other decisions are more difficult. For the couple's sake, parents and stepparents should lay aside personal feelings, and everyone should try to rally around on this special day and cooperate with the bride and groom's wishes.

BEFORE THE PROCESSIONAL

When a white carpet is used, it is rolled down the whole length of the aisle by two ushers. At some weddings, a broad, white ribbon is placed on the pew at each side of the aisle at the last moment. These rest folded on the last row of the reserved pews until the carpet is in place. Then two ushers walk with the ribbon from the front to the back of the church, draping them over the end of each row. They are not removed until the family and friends in the front reserved pews leave the church. This system allows the immediate family to leave quickly for the reception, before the rest of the guests are dismissed by the ushers pew by pew.

THE PROCESSIONAL

The bride and her father arrive on schedule just as the wedding is about to start. The procession forms in the vestibule. On signal, the clergymember followed by the groom and the best man assume their places in front of the altar at the right side of the altar; or in some churches, they stand at the top of the steps to the chancel. The best man stands slightly to the left behind the groom as they both face the congregation. As soon as they reach their places the procession starts down the aisle to the altar.

AT THE ALTAR

There is more than one way for attendants to stand at the altar. Usually this decision rests with the clergymember. Facing the altar, the maid or matron of honor stands to the bride's left. The flower girl stands behind the maid of honor, and the ring bearer stands behind the best man. The bridesmaids and ushers may pair up, or the bridesmaids may line up at a slight angle on one side and the ushers on the other. When the bride reaches the groom's side, she releases her father's arm, transfers her flowers to her left arm and gives her right hand to the groom. He puts it through his left arm and her hands rest near his elbow. Or the couple may simply stand side by side.

At this point in many ceremonies, the clergymember may ask, "Who gives this woman in holy matrimony?" to which the bride's father may answer, "We do," thus including the bride's mother. The father then takes his seat beside his wife. Now the couple approaches the altar and the bride hands the bouquet to her maid of honor.

The flower girl and trainbearers are usually seated after they have completed their part in the processional. Once the portion of the ceremony with the giving of the rings is completed, the ringbearer also may be seated.

Pledges of Parents

An affectionate alternative to the clergymember asking, "Who gives this woman in holy matrimony?" is to take note of the pledges of parents. We quote from the "United Methodist Service of Christian Marriage."

1) *Parents*   We rejoice in your union, and pray God's
              blessing upon you.

People	In the name of Jesus Christ we love you. By his grace, we commit ourselves with you to the bonds of marriage and the Christian home.
Minister	Will all of you, by God's grace, do everything in your power to uphold and care for these two persons in their marriage?
People	We will.
2) *Minister to parents*	Will you give your blessing to [bride] and [groom] in their new relationship? Will you support them with the love and freedom they need? Will you share your experience and wisdom with them as they seek it, as you learn from them as well?
Parents or	We will.
Parents	We now reaffirm our continuing love for our child, and we recognize that henceforth our primary responsibility is to both of them together.

THE WEDDING RING CEREMONY

The engagement ring is transferred to the ring finger of the right hand before the ceremony. After vows are exchanged, the best man produces the wedding ring to give to the minister or the groom. The maid of honor does the same with the groom's ring, if this is a double-ring ceremony. The minister blesses the bride's ring and gives it to the groom, who puts it on the bride's finger. He then blesses the groom's ring and gives it to the bride to put on the groom's finger. After the ceremony the bride transfers the engagement ring to her left hand.

THE WEDDING KISS

When a wedding kiss is included after the ceremony, the maid of honor lifts the bride's veil, if she is wearing one over her face, before the groom gives the bride a kiss. The bride receives the bouquet from the maid of honor and takes her husband's right arm and the recessional begins.

THE RECESSIONAL

The bride and groom are the first to go up the aisle, smiling happily at the congregation and followed in order by the attendants. The bride may stop to give her mother a flower and her father a kiss before leaving the sanctuary.

The ushers return to the reserved pews and escort the mothers and honored guests to the vestibule. They then remove the white ribbons and signal guests to leave their pews in sequence, starting from the front and moving to the back, until all guests have left.

FORMAL WEDDING PHOTOGRAPHS

The photographer takes pictures of the couple as they proceed up the aisle and as they emerge from the church. Sometimes, the bridal couple with the wedding party pose for formal pictures before leaving for the reception. Because this can take a very long time, I do not recommend it. From the guests' point of view there is much less delay when the formal wedding photographs are taken either before the ceremony or at the reception, right after the guests have gone through the receiving line.

This also allows the photographer to get to the reception site early and take prereception shots of the tables, the flowers, and the cake before guests arrive. So often the rush of many people obstructs the view of a beautifully decorated room.

WEDDING BELLS

Borrow the joyous English custom and let the church bells peal after the ceremony!

THE RECEIVING LINE

The place for the receiving line at the reception site should be carefully picked to avoid creating a bottleneck. It's much less confusing if a place is selected in advance instead of letting an impulsive line form which blocks an entrance or an exit. Allow plenty of room for a smooth, quick flow of guests, without delay. Make sure that there is a place for coats and boots for guests in wet weather. Coat racks can be rented from a party supply store.

The Bride and Groom Receive

No matter how informal the wedding, everyone still wants to greet the bride and groom personally, shake their hands, and wish them well. At very small informal weddings, when the bride and groom are hosts, they may receive congratulations from the guests by standing either at the exit after the ceremony or at the entrance to the reception. If they wish, the maid or matron of honor may stand near the groom and direct guests to the refreshment area.

The Couple and Their Parents Receive

The traditional receiving line starts with the bride's mother, followed by the groom's mother. However, if the reception is held in the groom's hometown, where his mother knows most of the guests by sight, it is better for her to be first in line.

The two fathers may also be in the receiving line next to their wives, but often they prefer to mingle with guests. In this case, the bride's father should introduce the groom's father to friends and vice versa.

The groom stands between his mother and the bride. The maid or matron of honor is next to the bride and last in line. She can graciously direct guests to the refreshment area. The bridesmaids are not usually in the receiving line, because this slows down the line for everyone. It's much more pleasant when the bridesmaids circulate among the guests in a friendly way. Young children are never expected to stand in a receiving line.

If members of the wedding party are wearing gloves, they may keep them on or take them off, as they wish.

At a large, very formal wedding, there may be an "announcer" standing next to the bride's mother. He asks each guest for his or her name and repeats this to the mother of the bride in case she hasn't met some of the guests invited by the groom's family.

It is not necessary to make clever conversation as one greets people in the receiving line. The bride and groom will tell everyone how glad they are to see them. The groom is congratulated, and the bride is offered best wishes. (The bride is never "congratulated.") Guests introduce themselves, if necessary, make a brief complimentary remark, and move on.

When there are many guests and a long line, it is perfectly all right for a guest to have a glass of champagne and circulate until the receiving line thins down. The empty glass is placed on a table before proceeding through the line.

The Bride's Father Receives

When the bride's father is not presently married and hosts a wedding, he stands first in the receiving line. Or he may invite the bride's aunt, grandmother, or any woman relative to receive with him.

Stepparents in the Receiving Line

When the bride or groom's parents are divorced and remarried, the stepparents do not appear in the receiving line, unless the stepparents host the wedding.

When There is No Receiving Line

When the wedding is very large with hundreds of people, it may be better to skip the receiving line altogether. In this case, the two sets of parents may station themselves in separate parts of the room and greet the guests informally. The bride and groom should make every effort to circulate among the guests and have a friendly word with everyone.

Or a warm friendly welcome may be extended over the public-address system.

THE GUEST BOOK

A valued memento of the occasion is to have a guest book available for everyone to sign. This book is placed on a table near the entrance or at the end of the receiving line. There are plumed pens available, which help call attention to the book. Any member of the family, friend, or bridesmaid may be asked to remind each guest to sign his or her name.

GIFTS BROUGHT TO THE RECEPTION

Some guests will bring gifts to the reception. A table for these gifts should be available, preferably near the entrance but in a secure place.

Someone should be designated to keep an eye on the gifts and gift cards and to transport them from the reception site to the couple's future home.

THE INFORMAL AFTERNOON RECEPTION

Chairs and tables are provided for everyone to sit wherever they please; refreshments are available; a little music fills the air, and the best man proposes the first toast. The wedding cake, the usual focal point, is the highlight of the occasion, and when it is time to cut the cake, guests are all notified and gather around to watch.

THE SEATED RECEPTION

Customs vary slightly in different parts of the country, but usually for a seated breakfast, brunch, luncheon, or dinner, there is a bride's table facing the room. The bride and groom sit at the center, with the maid of honor to the left of the groom, and the best man on the bride's right. The rest of the attendants and their husbands are also seated here, alternating men and women insofar as possible. One or two parents' tables may be placed near the bride's table where the clergyman and his wife and close relatives and friends are also seated.

An alternate arrangement is to seat the bride and groom, the clergyman and his wife, the parents and grandparents, the best man, and matron of honor at the bride's table.

The bride and groom are seated at their table either just before or just after the parents' table is seated. The couple may be introduced to the strains of "Here Comes the Bride" or other wedding music. A blessing or grace may be said before the meal is served.

Placecards at the Bride's Table

Placecards are a convenience that cuts down on confusion. "Where shall I sit?" and "Are you sitting here?" or "Why don't we sit there?"—all these questions can be avoided simply by using placecards.

They are used at the bride's table and at the parents' table, even when they are not used for all the seated guests. These special tables are served by waiters even when the rest of the guests serve themselves at a buffet.

Placecards should be legibly written in a dark green, blue, brown, or black shade of ink, so they are easy to read without glasses, especially in candlelight. Informal placecards are written with the first name only, or with the first and last name. For banquets or formal occasions the name is written out in full, as "Mrs. Loren Jay Lovejoy." They are placed directly above the plate at each place setting.

Placecards for Everyone

At very large formal luncheons or dinners, it's an advantage to use placecards in order to seat guests in congenial groups. When guests arrive at the door, they pick up an envelope with their names written on the outside. They check the table number that is written on a small card inside the envelope. They locate their table by number and seat themselves at the placecard with their name on it.

To organize the seating, a diagram is made up in advance, and each table is numbered, and every guest is assigned a place at a table. This diagram is clearly displayed behind the table where guests pick up their place cards. The cards are arranged alphabetically on one or more card tables. If there is more than one placecard table, each table is designated to handle a section of the alphabet, A–M, N–Z. Usually, couples are assigned to the same table but are not seated next to each other.

Again, this system cuts down on general confusion for all the guests and avoids people milling about wondering where to sit.

DANCING AT THE RECEPTION

The leader of the band often acts as master of ceremonies by signaling the beginning of the wedding dance formalities. If there is no band leader to assume this role, someone else should be put in charge, possibly the best man.

The first couple:	The bride and groom dance the first dance together.
The second couple:	The bride's father cuts in and dances with his daughter.
The third couple:	The groom asks the bride's mother to dance.
The fourth couple:	The groom's father cuts in on the bride.

The fifth couple:	The bride's father cuts in on the groom and dances with his wife.
The sixth couple:	The groom asks his mother to dance.

After a few minutes the band leader invites all the guests to dance.

At a formal sit-down dinner, the bride and groom usually start the dancing after the first course has been served.

TOASTS AT THE RECEPTION

At a seated luncheon or dinner, as soon as all the glasses are filled with wine and the guests have been served, the best man arises and makes the first toast to the couple. Other members of the bridal party join in proposing toasts, and the groom toasts his bride and his new in-laws.

When a toast is proposed to the bridal couple, everyone stands with the exception of the bride and groom.

CAKE-CUTTING CEREMONY

The cake-cutting ceremony at a sit-down meal takes place just before dessert is served.

The bride with the groom's hand over hers, cuts the first two slices. He offers her a bite of the first slice, and she offers him a bite of the second slice.

The photographer takes pictures, and someone steps in to continue cutting the cake, which is then served to all the guests. (If individual boxes of groom's cake are provided, guests will pick up their souvenirs as they leave the reception.)

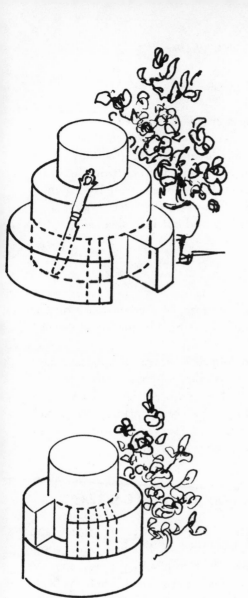

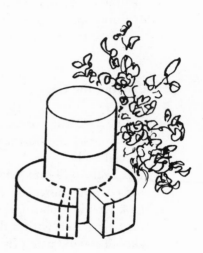

Cutting a Round Tiered Cake

(1) Starting with the bottom layer, cut medium-size slices up to the edge of the second layer. (2) When this is completed, start with the middle layer, cutting gradually all the way around the cake. (3) Now return to cutting the inner section of the bottom layer. (4) Remove the top layer (which is traditionally frozen to be eaten on the first anniversary); separate the remaining layers and cut into slices.

Cutting the Cake

The wedding cake may be used as a centerpiece on the bridal table, the buffet table, or it may be placed on its own special table.

A cake knife that is thin, sharp, or serrated should be used for cutting the cake. (An ordinary kitchen knife does not look well in a photograph.) If frosting sticks to the knife, it may be wiped with a damp paper towel after cutting each slice. To avoid using fingers, a cake server is also needed as a utensil for placing the piece of cake on the plate.

THROWING THE BOUQUET AND GARTER

This may be done either before or after the bride and groom change into their travel clothes. The bride and groom give the signal to the maid of honor and the best man to gather all the single men and women around. Then the bride throws her bouquet over her shoulder and the woman who catches it will become the next bride. The groom then throws the bride's garter to the bachelors in the crowd, and the man who catches it will become the next groom.

On the Day of the Wedding

TIME TO LEAVE

The bride and groom say goodbye to their parents and in-laws and thank the attendants privately, if they haven't already done so during the reception. As the bride and groom leave for their car, they may be showered with rose petals and good wishes for a long life of married bliss.

To give the bridal couple that comfortable feeling of being in control, a final checklist or countdown will help keep the time schedule running smoothly. A list of this kind may be run off on a duplicating machine, color coded, and shared with other members of the wedding party; caterer, florist, musicians, and photographer.

Here is a sample summary for a seven P.M. church wedding followed by a buffet dinner. The time and place may be changed, and the time span may be condensed or expanded as the case may be. For instance, a champagne and wedding cake reception may last only two hours, whereas a sit-down luncheon or dinner with music and dancing may last four hours.

LOVEJOY/BALDWIN WEDDING

Suggested Summary and Schedule

SATURDAY, JUNE 12, 7:00 P.M.

Ceremony _____
name of church

_____
address

219

Reception _____
                              hosted by

_____
                              name of site

_____
                              address

FRIDAY, JUNE 11, 6:00 P.M.

Rehearsal _____
                              name of church

_____
                              address

Rehearsal Dinner _____
                              hosted by

_____
                              name of site

_____
                              address

Memo: Bride and groom arrange to have their traveling clothes packed and delivered to reception site on Saturday by designated persons. Also arrange to have guestbook pen and souvenirs delivered to reception site. Arrange for a designated person to take programs and maps to church. Give rings to matron of honor and best man. Give gifts to attendants. Sign marriage certificate. Groom gives check to best man for clergyman.

SATURDAY, JUNE 12

4:30 P.M. Attendants and parents are present at the bride's home to wait for the photographer to take candids. (A tray of sandwiches is available.)
Florist arrives with bouquets, corsages, and headpieces for women and a boutonniere for bride's father.

4:45 P.M. Photographer arrives to take pictures of wedding party and family.

5:00 P.M. Florist delivers flowers and boutonnieres for ushers at the church.
Caterer begins setting up for reception at reception site.

5:30 P.M. Ushers arrive at church and pin on boutonnieres. They receive final instructions regarding programs, maps, and seating guests.

6:00 P.M. Three cars are available at the bride's home.
Groom and best man arrive at church in best man's car.

6:10 P.M. Photographer arrives at church to take candid shots of groom, groomsmen, and parents.
Florist arrives at reception site with flowers and floral ornament for cake.

6:15 P.M. Musicians arrive at church.
Car #1 leaves bride's home with bridesmaids.
Car #2 leaves bride's home with mother of the bride, matron of honor, and grandparents.

221

6:20 P.M.   Car #3 leaves bride's home with bride and her father.

6:30 P.M.   Ushers prepare to seat guests, hand out programs.
Prelude music begins.

6:40 P.M.   Entire wedding party is in the vestibule of the church.
Altar candles are lit.

6:50 P.M.   Ushers seat groom's mother and grandparents.

6:58 P.M.   Mother of the bride is seated by a designated usher.

7:00 P.M.   Wedding solo is sung.

7:05 P.M.   Ceremony begins.

FOLLOWING THE CEREMONY:

Car #1 drives the bride and groom to the reception.
Car #2 transports parents of the bride and grandparents to the reception.
Car #3 transports the bridesmaids to the reception.
Best man escorts the matron of honor to reception in his car.
Ushers will transport guests without transportation to the reception.

7:30 P.M.   Valet parkers arrive at reception site.

7:45 P.M.   Musicians will be ready to play.
Bar will open and waiters are prepared to serve champagne on trays as guests arrive.

7:50 P.M.   Receiving line forms.

8:00 P.M.   Hors d'oeuvres are passed.

8:30 P.M.   Photographer takes formal photographs of wedding party.

8:45 P.M. Bride and groom lead the first dance and the traditional dance sequence follows:

The bride's father comes to the floor and dances with his daughter.

The groom asks the bride's mother to dance.

The groom's father comes to the floor and dances with the bride.

The bride's father cuts in on the groom and dances with his wife.

The groom dances with his mother.

After a few moments, the orchestra leader invites guests to join the family on the dance floor.

9:00 P.M. Buffet supper is served.

9:30 P.M. Bride, groom, and best man proceed to cake table. Here three glasses of champagne are waiting. The best man proposes a toast. The groom may respond if he wishes. Other guests may also propose toasts at this time. The bride and groom cut the first slice of cake. The photographer takes pictures and then the waiters cut and serve the cake to the guests.

10:15 P.M. The best man announces that the bride is about to throw her bouquet. The single men and women gather around. After tossing the bouquet (and garter) the couple leave the reception to change their clothes.

They return to say good-bye, possibly having a last dance before leaving. The bridesmaids distribute rose petals to the guests, who throw them after the departing couple.

Memo: The bride's parents, with the help of other members of the wedding party or close friends, are responsible for gathering the bride's wedding attire, the top of the wedding cake, guestbook, flowers, and gifts and transporting them to a predesignated place. They thank the caterer and musicians.

The groom has made arrangements for someone to see that all the men's rented wedding clothes including his own are returned promptly to the rental store.

THE AFTERGLOW

Sometime after the reception, either on the same day or on the following day, the wedding party and members of the family and close friends often split into little groups to enjoy reviewing the preceding events. This exchange may take place in someone's kitchen, around a swimming pool, or even while driving to the airport. But wherever or whenever, reminiscing can be one of the most heartwarming and rewarding experiences of the wedding.

Who hasn't shared a chuckle over the almost-happenings or mis-happenings? Oh dear, someone forgot to pick up grandmother at the beauty parlor and she almost missed the wedding! Or who hasn't become misty eyed when observing the unexpected sentimentality of the groom's father, who cried at the rehearsal! Or who hasn't sighed with relief to find an accommodating choir boy with the right gadget to unlock the bride's mother's car door when her keys were inadvertently locked inside. Or who wouldn't be jumpy recalling the episode when the puppy carried off the flower girl's shoe.

If the newlyweds plan a delayed honeymoon, they may even share in the afterglow and enjoy opening the gifts that were brought to the reception. Such a very informal, unprogrammed, shoes-off kind of gathering helps everyone to unwind and is essential in helping with the ticklish transition for those who have devoted so much time and energy in planning the wedding to a return to the normal routine of everyday life.

THE HONEYMOON

Some couples plan a weekend honeymoon, and some plan a month-long honeymoon. And some plan a delayed honeymoon. For the latter, it may be more practical to settle into the new apartment or house after the wedding until both are able to take their vacations at a convenient later date.

The choice of a place should be considered very carefully—it should be an area that both the bride and groom will enjoy. As the saying goes, "What this country needs is an ocean in the mountains." Be that as it may, what really counts when choosing a honeymoon site is to talk to people who have been there and to people whose views you share. Don't be afraid to ask a lot of questions about where to stay, what the place has to offer, where to eat, and what to wear at this time of year. It's good to know that you never need a raincoat in California during the summer months, but you always need a sweater in the northern half of the United States.

Make it a point to find out in advance the kinds of things there are to do after you arrive and what they cost. Are there free concerts in the park? Free museum tours? Public beaches? Art fairs? State fairs? Free industrial tours? Good public transportation? If one is centrally located one may save money on transportation that can be added to the price of the room. Check with the local newspaper or magazine or write to the Chamber of Commerce. It pays to shop around with more than one travel agency.

Decide if you prefer to spend your honeymoon in posh accommodations in isolated surroundings, depending on good books and records for entertainment, or if you would like to land in the middle of a major city with elegant restaurants, theaters and shops. Or is camping in the mountains by a trout stream your idea of heaven—or sailing on blue lakes?

If one of you gets seasick, don't choose a cruise! Or if one of you is fair-skinned, avoid tropical sunshine.

Finally, a honeymoon doesn't have to be a twosome the whole time. It's possible to make friends while you are on your honeymoon. It's up to you to ask people to join you for a meal or share a sightseeing trip together. Sometimes lifelong friends are made this way. When you return from your honeymoon, rested and eager to settle in your new home, you will want to call your friends and relatives over for coffee and tell them about your trip. It's the very beginning of a new social life together.

APPENDIX

Customs, Traditions, and Superstitions

There's a time to wink
as well as a time to see.

BEN FRANKLIN

Why do brides wear white? Why does the best man dress like the groom? Who started the curious practice of throwing rice at weddings? Why do the bride and bridegroom find it necessary to sneak away after the wedding? And why do people play practical jokes on newlyweds?

THE FIRST STAGE OF MARRIAGE CUSTOMS

In tracing the origins of marriage customs, we find the marriage ceremony has progressed through three general stages. Originally marriages were consummated by force, the groom capturing a desirable woman, often of another tribe. The "best man" is the modern counterpart of the fellow-warrior, who helped the bridegroom capture and carry off the bride.

The Origin of the Honeymoon

This goes back to the days when the bridegroom found it necessary to hide his prize until her family grew tired of searching for her.

Over the Threshold

Today, carrying the bride over the threshold symbolizes the groom's conquest by force. It is also said by some scholars that the groom is following a good-luck custom possibly originating with the Romans, who felt the evil spirits were thus kept away from the new home.

The Wedding Veil

The Romans also believed that demon spirits were jealous of peoples' happiness, and since weddings are joyful events, it was necessary to confuse the devil. It was for this reason that brides wore veils to throw the devil off the track.

Dressing Alike

In order to deceive the devil, bridal couples were surrounded by friends who all dressed alike.

Teasing

Because it was considered dangerous for lovers to be happy, it became customary to tease the bride and groom, to hide their belongings, and to be the targets for friendly abuse. A good example of this teasing is still practiced today with the *shivaree*. The *shivaree* is a noisy mock serenade held late during the wedding night to harass the newlyweds. This early Latin custom was introduced in America by the French people of Canada and Louisiana.

Throwing Rice

If the devil could be convinced that mortals are truly miserable, it was believed he would consider it a waste of energy to add any supernatural punishments. If all else failed, it was believed possible to buy off cantankerous spirits by throwing a few handfuls of rice.

THE SECOND STAGE OF MARRIAGE CUSTOMS

This was marriage by contract or purchase, which lasted in England as late as the middle of the sixteenth century. The Anglo-Saxon word "wed" originally meant the purchase money or its equivalent in horses, cattle, or other property that the groom gave the father of the bride to seal the transaction.

THE THIRD STAGE OF MARRIAGE CUSTOMS

Marriage by mutual love evolved gradually. There was a period in time during the Roman Republic that the marriage ceremony was a solemn religious ordinance. Later, under the Roman Empire, however, religion fell into contempt and marriage became virtually a civil contract. By slow degrees, Christianity gave marriage back its religious character as couples paired off together to ask for the blessing of their pastor. It was not until the Council of Trent in 1563 that the Catholic church made it mandatory for a marriage to be performed by a priest in the presence of two or three witnesses. Subsequently, marriage continued to be regarded as a divine institution until the French Revolution when the new Constitution made civil marriage mandatory in 1791.

The Engagement Ring

The gift of a ring is a very old custom which was used to seal any important or sacred agreement.

"And Pharoah said unto Joseph,
See I have set thee over all the land of Egypt.
And Pharoah took off his ring from his hand, and
put it upon Joseph's hand."

(GENESIS X:41–42.)

A Greek engagement or betrothal ring of the fourth century
B.C. bears the following inscription, "To her who excels not
only in virtue and prudence, but also in wisdom."

The Hope Chest

The idea of the "hope chest" grew out of the ancient
custom of the dowry, which in turn grew out of the much
older custom of marriage by purchase.

The Trousseau

The word *trousseau* originated from the word *trusse*, meaning
a little bundle.

Courting by the American Indian

Among the North American Indians, it was customary for
a young brave to present gifts not to the girl, but to her
father. If the gifts were accepted, the betrothal was considered sealed.

Circumcision as a Prerequisite to Marriage

There is undoubtedly magic significance to the importance
of circumcision not only among the Jews, Mohammedans,
and some members of Christian sects, but also among the
natives of the West Coast of Africa, the Kafirs, the aborigines
of Australia, and nearly all the peoples of Eastern and Cen-

Customs, Traditions, and Superstitions

tral Africa, Madagascar, Melanesia, the Indian Archipelago, and Polynesia, and many of the Indian tribes of the Western Hemisphere. Circumcision is conceded to be the oldest surgical operation, and it is the only one still having a religious significance, or considered to be a prerequisite to marriage.

Bundling

Bundling was an old New England custom introduced by the Dutch and the English which permitted engaged couples to lie in bed together without undressing during long, cold winter evenings.

Spooning

In Wales, a man would often carve a spoon from a piece of wood with his pocket knife. This would be attached to a ribbon and worn by a girl around her neck as a sign of their engagement. The expression "spooning," meaning to court or go steady, originated from this custom.

The Marriage Season

In Morocco marriages are generally celebrated in autumn at the close of the harvest season, when grainaries are full of corn. But most European countries follow the Roman tradition of holding weddings in spring, when homage was paid to the three major divinities: Ceres, Maia, and Flora.

The Bachelor Dinner

This custom is believed to have originated in Sparta, where the bridegroom entertained his friends at supper on the eve of the wedding. This event was known as the "men's mess."

On the Wedding Day

One marriage taboo was that the bride should not see or talk to the groom before the ceremony on the day of the wedding. This practice is being completely ignored today.

The Wedding Ring

The wedding ring is believed to have evolved from the engagement ring. The earliest record appears in Egyptian hieroglyphics, where a circle represents eternity. According to tradition, early Hebrew wedding rings were usually plain gold, silver, or base metal without any setting. Even wood, rush, and leather were sometimes used in olden times. Apparently, Jewish wedding rings were of a ceremonial nature because they were often too large to wear on the finger. The use of the wedding ring among Christians has been traced back to the year 860. It is said that when a marriage settlement was properly sealed, rings bearing the names of the newly married couple were passed around for inspection among the guests. The wedding ring is placed on the third finger of the left hand because it was believed this finger is connected directly to the heart by the "vena amoris" or vein of love. But most fingers of both hands, including the thumb, have been used for wedding rings in the past. During the Elizabethan period in England, the wedding ring was worn on the thumb, as is shown in oil paintings of ladies of that time. In traditional Jewish weddings the ring is placed on the first finger of the left hand.

The Wedding Gown

The bridal gown as we know it today was first introduced by Empress Eugenie, a leader of fashion. She wore the white gown at her wedding to Napoleon III, who ruled France from 1853 to 1871.

The Bridal Wreath

The custom of wearing a wreath of orange blossoms was introduced in Europe by the Crusaders. Orange blossoms were also carried by brides in their bouquets as a symbol of fertility. In Norway the bride always wears a wreath of white flowers. After the wedding ceremony she is blindfolded and surrounded by a circle of her bridesmaids. She then dances a folk dance alone and gives the wreath to one of the maids, who according to old legend will be the first to wed. The wreath is passed to each bridesmaid who then steps out of the circle. The game ends when the last bridesmaid receives the wreath.

Good Luck Symbols

Most brides like to follow the superstition that they must wear "something old, something new, something borrowed, and something blue" for good luck. Another popular wedding custom is to distribute sugar-coated almonds to all guests. This souvenir is called *confetti* by Italians and represents the bitterness and sweetness of life. The almonds are attractively wrapped in tulle and tied with a ribbon.

Wedding Cake

The modern wedding cake is probably directly descended from the Roman *conferreatio*, a particular kind of cake which was broken on the bride's head as a symbol of fruitfulness and plenty. Each guest took a piece of this cake home. The survival of this custom continues with what is nowadays called the groom's cake, which is neatly boxed for guests to take with them from the reception. A modern day custom is to remove the small top layer of the wedding cake and keep it in the freezer to be shared by the couple on their first anniversary.

Toasting Custom

Toasting comes from an ancient French custom of placing a piece of bread in the bottom of a glass; a good toaster drained the drink to get the "toast." An old English toast goes like this:

> Love, be true to her; Life, be dear to her;
> Health, stay close to her; Joy, draw near to her;
> Fortune, find what you can do for her,
> Search your treasure-house through for her,
> follow her footsteps, the wide world over,
> And keep her husband always her lover!

The Kiss

The Scotch in particular were greatly impressed with the importance of the bridal kiss. Quoting from an old Scottish source, "the parson who presided over the marriage ceremony uniformly claimed it as his inaniable privilege to have a smack at the lips of the bride immediately after the performance of his official duties."

The Dollar Dance

In some communities, guests who dance with the bride or groom at the reception are required to pay a dollar for each dance. A variation of this custom is for guests to put money or checks in a small white satin purse the bride wears on her wrist.

Throwing Shoes

The Assyrians and Hebrews gave a sandal as a token of good faith when closing a bargain or to signify the transfer of property. The Egyptians exchanged sandals to indicate a transfer of property or granting authority. It was customary to fling a sandal to the ground as a symbol of possession of the land.

Upon the land of Edom do I cast my shoe.

PSALMS 60:8; 108:9

In old Britain it was customary for the father to give his new son-in-law one of the bride's shoes, in token of the transfer of authority, and the bride was tapped on the head with the shoe to impress her with her husband's new authority and position. However, the husband was obliged to take an oath to treat his wife well.

Decorating Cars

Old shoes trailing the bridal get-away car is a dying custom, but signs, balloons, and streamers are still popular.

Wedding Presents

According to an etiquette book published in 1907 by the New York Society of Self-Culture, "wedding presents have now, in some instances, become almost gorgeous. The old fashion started amongst the frugal Dutch with the custom of providing the young couple with their household gear and a sum of money with which to begin their married life. It has now degenerated into a very bold display of wealth and ostentatious generosity, so that friends of moderate means are afraid to send anything. . . . In France they do things better—the nearest of kin subscribing a sum of money which is sent to the bride's mother, who invests it in good securities, in gold and silver, in the bridal trousseau, or in the furnishing of the house, as the good sense of all parties combines to direct."

CONCLUSION

We thought it would be fun to share with you the origins of some of the customs, traditions and superstitions that began thousands of years ago, many of which remain with us until today. From all we've read, undoubtedly there is a mystique lovers require when exchanging vows and the degree of the mystique varies from individual to individual. Much depends, naturally, on the couple's environment and family upbringing. For some couples, a civil ceremony in the judge's chambers is quite enough. For others, the simple Quaker ceremony witnessed by friends is sufficiently meaningful. Some couples feel that the warmth and familiarity of a home or garden wedding is the only way to go, while other young couples believe deeply they wouldn't be married unless they walk down the aisle together in a church. Whatever the custom or tradition in your family, the important thing is for you to follow your dream, to be comfortable with your decisions, to be considerate of each other's feelings, to hold fast to your beliefs, and to act kindly toward your family and friends. The ethnic customs and family traditions you choose to follow will make your wedding uniquely your own.

REFERENCE BOOKS

Arisian, Khoran. *The New Wedding/Creating Your Own Marriage Ceremony.* New York: Vintage Books, 1973. (Paperback)

Brown, Gail, and Dillon, Karen Horton. *How to Sew Your Own Wedding Dress.* Portland, Oregon: Palmer/Pletsch Associates. (Paperback)

Burk, Tom. *How to Photograph Weddings, Groups & Ceremonies.* Tucson: HP Books.

Center For A Woman's Own Name. Booklet for women who wish to determine their own names after marriage. 261 Kimberley, Barrington, Ill. 60010. (Paperback) $3.00 includes postage and handling.

Crowley, Jerry. *The Fine Art of Garnishing.* Baltimore: Lieba Inc. (Tools are available with this book.)

Index

Best man (*continued*)
  duties of, 115–16
  in Jewish ceremony, 193–94
  in processional, 186–87
  in recessional, 192
  at seated reception, 213–14
  toasts and, 116, 216
Betrothal, Office of, 197
Beverages, 69, 72–78
  at brunches, 79
Birthstone rings, 17, 19
Bouquets. *See* Flowers
Boutonnieres, 117, 148
Bridal
  fashion shows, 124
  gown, 123–26, 234
    flowers and, 144–46
    preserving, 126
  salons, 125
  showers, 24–27
  wreath, 235
Bride
  at altar, 207
  bridal showers and, 26
  calendar for, 42–45
  in Catholic ceremony, 200
  dancing and, 215–16
  in Eastern Orthodox ceremony,
    197
  expenses for, 39
  flowers for, 140, 141, 207, 209,
    217
    bridal gown and, 144–46
  giving away of, 188
  in Jewish ceremony, 193–94
  in processional, 187
  in Quaker ceremony, 197–98
  in receiving line, 210–12
  at seated reception, 213–14
Bride's cake. *See* Cake
Bride's father. *See* Father(s)
Bridesmaids, 116–17, 203–04
  at altar, 207

in Catholic ceremony, 200
dress for, 128–29
duties of, 117
expenses for, 40
flowers for, 117, 141, 146–48
junior, 114, 118, 128
parties, 27–28
in processional, 187
in receiving line, 211
in recessional, 192
Bride's mother. *See* Mother(s)
Broken engagement, 23–24
Brown, Gail, 124
Browning, Robert, 137
Brunches, 31, 79–80
Budget, 37–45
  dress and, 11
  expenses and, 39–41
  wedding coordinator and, 41–42
  See also Fees
Buffet, 63–65, 80
Bundling, 233

Cake, 66–68, 235
  -cutting ceremony, 216–18
  groom's, 67–68, 235
Calendar; bride and groom's,
  42–45
Calligraphy, for invitations, 88
Calling cards, 103
Canapes, 78–79
Cancellations, 56
Candid photographs, 163
Candlelight ceremony, 118–19
Cards, 101–08, 214–15
  acknowledgment, 106–08
  insert, 101–04
  missing from gifts, 174
Caron, Allan, 157
Carpet, white, 118, 206
Carroll, Lewis, 83
Cars, decorating, 237

Honeymoon, 224–26
  origin of, 229
Honor roles, 9–10
Hope chest, 232
Hors d'ouevres, hot, 79
Hyphenated names, 109

"Ich liebe dich" (song), 157
Indians, American, courting of, 232
Infants, at church ceremony, 55
Informal
  dress, 10–11, 134
  weddings, 87, 114–16, 133
Informals (stationery), 86, 106
In-house consultants, 41–42
Inscriptions on rings, 17–18
Insert cards, 101–04
Insurance for rings, 18
Invitations, 85–104
  abbreviations on, 92, 93
  addressing, 85–86, 91–92
  artwork for, 88
  cohosts and, 99
  crest on, 90
  for double weddings, 100
  mailing of, 43, 91
  ordering of, 88–92
  for receptions, 101–02, 109–10
  for second marriages, 96, 101
  for showers, 27
  styles of, 86–87
  wording of, 92–104
    parents and, 98–99
    titles in, 96–98

"Jesu, Joy of Man's Desiring" (song), 158
Jewish ceremony, 192–96
  dates for, 52–53
Johnson, Lyndon B., 35

Joint checking account, 24
Junior bridesmaids, 114, 118, 128

Kiss, wedding, 209, 236

Leave-taking, 219
Lettering, raised, 90
License, marriage, 114, 115, 192
Lifestyle, gift registry and, 171–72
Limousine rental, 180
Liquor, 69, 72, 74–77, 78
Lohengrin (opera), 157
"Longer" (song), 158
"Lord's Prayer, The" (song), 157
Luncheons, 31, 68, 80–81

Machine engraving, 90
Maid/Matron of honor, 209, 217
  at altar, 207
  in Catholic ceremony, 200
  dress for, 128
  duties of, 114–15
  flowers for, 148
  in Jewish ceremony, 193
  in processional, 187
  in receiving line, 210–11
  in recessional, 192
  at seated reception, 213–14
Makeup, 165–66
"Marche Nuptiale," 157
Marriage customs. *See* Customs
Marriage
  license, 114, 115, 192
  season, 233
Marriage, second. *See* Second marriages
Married name, 108–09
Mass, nuptial, 199–200
Mendelssohn, Felix, 157, 158
Men's wear. *See under* Dress

MORE IMPORTANT BOOKS FROM WARNER